TALES FROM THE ZIRZAMEEN

by

Brian Hanson Appleton aka Rasool Aryadust

TATE PUBLISHING
AND ENTERPRISES, LLC

The events, people, and places herein are depicted to the best recollection of the author, who assumes complete and sole responsibility for the accuracy of this narrative.

Published by Tate Publishing & Enterprises, LLC
127 E. Trade Center Terrace | Mustang, Oklahoma 73064 USA
1.888.361.9473 | www.tatepublishing.com

Tate Publishing is committed to excellence in the publishing industry. The company reflects the philosophy established by the founders, based on Psalm 68:11,
"The Lord gave the word and great was the company of those who published it."

Book design copyright © 2014 by Tate Publishing, LLC. All rights reserved.

Published in the United States of America

ISBN: 978-1-63268-965-8
1. Biography & Autobiography / Cultural Heritage
2. History / Middle East / Iran
14.04.02

Dedication

I would like to dedicate this book to my mother,
Lily Beth Appleton,
who has always believed in my dreams...

and

to my wife, Laura Scott Clow,
for her encouragement and
her P.R. abilities....

CONTENTS

PREFACE

Forty Days in the Wilderness of Heartland

With my heart full of love beyond the breaking point
I lay my youthful head in Leila's waiting lap
The familiar scent of her like tuber roses
I breathe in long and deep.

Safely wrapped in her arms and legs, I surrender
To sweet dreams of bright tomorrow
with her fair turquoise gemstone
and I, old silver in betrothal ring
of life promised together.

Under cover of full darkness,
the moon loses her shyness coming out to play....
Kneeling over me, she gently kisses my eyelids into sleep, perhaps trance,
Resisting, I long to bury my face in her full snow white bosom.
Her soft black hair tickles my face, gazing at me with silent burning desire
like still waters running deep, but I am too tired to raise my head.

Twenty seven days later, I awake alone, wandering in the Lut Desert,
following the tracks of her camel endlessly to the West.
Where are my cucumbers and melons, grapes and dates?
No figs, no cherries, no eggplants, no pomegranates.
Here there is only hot sand scalding my feet.
What has become of her my youth, my one true love, where is she now?
Like saffron's mother crocuses waiting beneath spring snow will she

Come out again to bloom on the 40th day of Lent and
Shower me with a 100,001 stolen kisses
While jealous bearded deities above
Are not looking?

And is her name Iran…
Or am I destined
For madness?

—Majnun

INTRODUCTION

For Love of Persia

SINCE THE AGE OF SIXTEEN IN 1966 UNTIL THE PRESENT DAY I HAVE BEEN a lover of Persian culture and language. I went to Iran for the first time when I was sixteen as the houseguest of an old aristocratic family who could trace both sides of their family back one thousand years and showed me titles and land grants given to their ancestors by Nader Shah.

I went to school in Rome, Italy, for five years with one of their sons who started teaching me Farsi in exchange for English, but he also taught me much, much more than just the language. He taught me about the proverbs, the taroff (honorifics), the poems, the cuisine, the jokes, the Mullah Nazrudin stories, the sweets and candies and confections like the pistachios, the dates, and the melon, sun flower and pumpkin seeds (Persians are big time seed eaters shelling them neatly and in rapid succession between their teeth until the floors of the movie theatres were full of husks) and a whole Persian world view: the generosity of Persian friendship, the elaborate system of good manners, how to show respect to elders, to statesmen, how to recognize the humanity in everyone from the humblest to the greatest.

He taught me many things, like giving other people presents when you had some great success as a way of sharing your good fortune and not making them jealous of it. Next thing you know, I found myself bickering over who should go through the door first or who should pay the restaurant bill. The concept of dividing up the bill evenly between us was unthinkable and un-Iranian. Over the course of time I figured out that, although it took longer, having each person take turns paying the entire restaurant bill eventually evened out, the same as dividing up each bill but with two added advantages: Each of us got to play the big shot in public and this arrangement tended to help sustain friendships because in order to get paid back you had to keep going out to dinner with the same people. This was a completely foreign language in itself to your average American.

The Iranians had a wonderful quality which, having grown up in Italy, I had also seen in the Italian culture, which was the appreciation of the individual with all his eccentricities, strengths, and flaws, the great human interest that people took in what made an individual interesting or amusing or unique. There was no total reliance on technology, or trends, or fashion, or the opinions of others, or the size of someone's wallet or car or house to define who they were.

Although many of the newly wealthy cared about fashion, street addresses, and club memberships, when I went to live in Iran in 1974, I went into a world where not only the wealthy would shower a visitor with generosity but even the poorest individual would try to give you the shirt off his back or cook for you his last chicken. It was a world where rich and famous people spent as much time talking about the latest misadventure of one of their servants, or trying to get their servant married off properly, or trying to help him earn some extra money by finding him outside jobs working a friend's party or a government function, as they spent time talking about their own children, friends, and affairs.

I found a world where the neighborhood car washer who lived in the street was someone everybody knew and gave gifts to on Aid-e-Gorban (a Shiite tithing holiday). In fact our neighborhood car washer was named Lolahozi. I never saw a beggar in that Iran. No matter how poor a person was, he would be selling something, even if it was only pencils or gerdou (brine pickled walnuts.) I found a world where family elders would still help settle the marital disputes of their children and nephews and nieces.

I found a world where everyone was in charge and no one was a subordinate, which made organizing anything, even something as simple as the tenants of a six-unit apartment building trying to collect the money to buy another tank of heating fuel, almost impossible, and yet it was a world where humanity was the measuring stick. I learned the meaning of: "What is possible everywhere else in the world is impossible in Iran, but what is impossible everywhere else in the world is possible in Iran." I could give many examples but two will suffice. My very first day on a new job with a large American corporation, my boss's younger brother, who was about eighteen at the time, had gotten arrested the night before for drunk and disorderly conduct at the Pars American Club, ultimately getting into a fist fight with a local policeman and throwing him into the swimming pool until reinforcements arrived. I was asked by my boss to go down to the police station and see what it would take to get his brother released. This was my first day on the job and, never having dealt with the police in Iran, I was a bit nervous about the outcome—and besides I did not particularly admire his brother's behavior to begin with. On my way by taxi, I began to fabricate a story for Tony which would appeal to the Iranian sensibility.

I explained to the chief of the police station that Tony had gotten a little carried away last night with the partying because he had just become engaged to be married to an Iranian girl whose parents had consented. In fact Tony actually did end up marrying an Iranian girl but several years later. The police chief, upon hearing this explanation, seemed to be satisfied and sympathetic, so I took the next venture, which was to ask him what I could do to obtain his release from jail. The police chief called in the policeman who had been hit and thrown in the pool by Tony and told me to ask him what I could do. The policeman listened politely to my explanation of Tony's behavior and then, in a very modest and friendly way, he showed me his torn uniform and said that since he had to pay for his own uniform, if I could just pay for the repair of his uniform, which was probably less than ten dollars, he would be satisfied—provided, of course, that Tony didn't get into anymore fights. And so I left with Tony next to me in my taxi that very afternoon, which was not the outcome I had expected.

Can you imagine what would have happened to an Iranian who had gotten drunk in some private club in the USA and struck a policeman and thrown him in the swimming pool back in 1974? He would probably still be serving time in jail to this day.

The other story I want to tell is how one of the supervisors of the American corporation for which I worked was rear ended by an Iranian workman on his motorcycle one morning on the way to work. The American supervisor had been put in jail—not the guilty party who had rear ended his car and who was driving his motorcycle without a license. I understood by this time that the police, other than the highest-ranking ones, considered themselves to be working class as well and they always seemed to favor who ever was poorer rather than whose fault it was. The American did not understand this unwritten, unspoken concept at all, and of course he didn't understand a word of Farsi either, even though he had lived there for years, so his reaction was to scream and yell and bang on the walls of his cell and make gigantic threats about what his embassy was going to do about this injustice when he got out of jail.

By this time I had learned the routine. I asked the judge how much the repair bill on the motorcycle was going to be, and when he told me some modest sum like one hundred fifty or two hundred dollars, I started to hand it over to the motorcycle driver. I had one condition that I addressed to the judge and to the policemen present: that they keep the loud-mouthed American supervisor for a few days rather than turning him loose immediately.

They had no problem with my request. This is a true story, one of many I want to tell you. I became so Iranianized over the course of the next 5 years that I became a Moslem at the Tehran Rotary Club in the presence of the late Foreign Minister Ghallatbari, the late Prime Minister Manucher Eghbal's younger brother Khosro, and many other dignitaries of the Shah's government. The priest presiding over the ceremony was Imam Jomeh, the Shah's personal priest. It was in the local papers and I still have copies of the articles and photographs from that ceremony. I adopted the pseudonym Rasool Aryadust on that occasion, which was the name my friend's father Alia had chosen for me for the event.

In addition I became a very good friend of Professor Parvin Ansary, who is a film producer and director who lives in Rome and was good friends with the lates: Fellini, Vittorio Di Sica, Vittorio Gazman, Anna Maria Pier Angeli, Paul Bartel, Marcello Mastroiani, and comedian Alberto Sordi, and still live Sofia Loren and many other Italian actors, directors and producers, such as: Antonioni, Visconti, Bertolucci, and Gian Maria Volonte, as well as Iranians such as Kimiyaee, Abassi and Kimiavi, and many more. Khanoum-e-Parvin put me in two of her films in Iran, which both the Italian and Iranian National TV and radio companies helped to subsidize. I played the role of Sir Robert Shirley, who was an historic character, in one of the films set in the Safavid time of Shah Abbas. I met the then-current TV starlet Atesh in that film and acted with her, sometimes in my role or more often as the double of her Italian husband in the film because the real life actor couldn't ride a horse or row a boat or any of those manly things. We even had use of the Shah's horses for one of the scenes in the film. Another role was given to Nakhshineh in this film, who later went on to become the Dai Jan Napolon of the extremely popular local TV series adapted from Iraj Pezeshkhzad's novel of the same name: *My Uncle Napoleon*. Our film *The Travels of Pietro Della Valle* went on to win a gold medal at the Nice Documentary Film Festival that year.

I have photos of all these people and of the filmings, which I would like to share with you later in this book. In our second film I got to know Shohreh Aghdashlou, who was wonderful and fun to work with, and I had the incredible experience of re-introducing myself to her backstage after a production of *Our Share of Father's House* September 9, 2001, at a college campus theatre in Northern California after we had not seen each other since 1977 or '78 in Iran. Three years ago she played a significant role in Steven Spielberg's film *The House of Sand and Fog*, for which she was nominated for an Oscar for Best Supporting Actress.

The real purpose of this collection of short stories, however, is to honor all my Persian friends, such as Professor Parvin Ansary for her art films. She has really made a great, often behind-the-scenes contribution and effect on Iranian cinema and theatre, and she should be recognized by her own compatriots as much as she is in the annals of Hollywood and Cine Citta. I also wish to honor Persian culture and help to create a better understanding and a bridge between our countries.

CHAPTER ONE

A Mid Summer Night's Dream amid the Jasmine

IT WAS THE SUMMER OF 1966. I WAS "SIXTEEN AND NEVER BEEN kissed." I was landing in the darkness by myself at Mehrabad airport for the first time in my life, having flown that day from Rome to meet my schoolmate Touss, named after the birthplace of Ferdowsi. I was going to spend the summer with him and his family and I didn't know what to expect.

I was a little nervous when I saw an absolute wall of people with their faces pressed to the glass wall outside the arrival concourse, and I was wondering how I was going to find my friend. Suddenly a huge cry rose up and a certain section of that wall began waving and undulating distinctly from the rest of the crowd. An entire clan, complete with a small army of servants and former servants and neighbors, a bus driver former servant, a gigantic former chauffeur, and the neighborhood barber had all been sent out to meet me.

In a matter of minutes I was kissed and hugged more times than I can count by people I had never met before, both men and women and children. My bags were taken from me and I was practically carried to the car. We sped through the streets of Tehran, passing Mehdineh Valliad, where a huge line of people were waiting to see *How the West Was Won* starring Jimmy Stewart. When we got to Touss's house on Kuche Goharshad, it was quite dark and I couldn't really see much except that all the rooms seemed to open onto a courtyard with a loggia around it where there were quite a few people sleeping on mattresses because it was cooler outdoors. Touss's mom, who was tall and thin and as beautiful and exotic looking as Queen Nefertiti of ancient Egypt, welcomed me with open arms and in her voice, which was warm as honey and sounded like the purring of a cat, asked me if I wanted a hamburger for dinner.

I told her I did not have to have American food, although she was very kind to offer, but that I would like to try everything Iranian that they ate. She

1

made me some cotlet that night, but from then forward she and Roya, the cook, made sure that I had something Persian and different every day, from dom balon (Rocky Mountain oysters), gigar (sheep's liver), margz (sheep's brains), Kookoo Sabzi (spinach omelet four inches high), Zaboon (sheep's tongue), and Kuft-e-Tabrizi (giant meatball), to Kalam Pache (sheep head and feet) on the hilltop with the sunrise. We even had noon-e-barbari (unleavened bread) toasted on top of the *bokhari* (kerosene space heater) and then stuffed with caviar for breakfast. I learned to drink cardamom flavored tea from little gold rimmed glasses, taking the sugar cubes into my teeth and sipping the tea through them, the same way my Russian great-grandmother had done, and I learned the joys of *shirini* (pastry) and candies like Nogl (rose water flavored candy) and Gaz (pistachio nougat) as well as *faloodeh* (Persian ice cream.) But my all time favorite dessert was Yakht dar Behesht (Ice in Paradise). There was also a wonderful drink, which was essentially a Persian melon smoothie. Speaking of *kharboseh* (Persian melons), during the years I ended up living in Iran, whenever I was down in morale, all I had to do was eat a nice cold Persian melon and I would feel better no matter what was bothering me. When they were out of season I was out of sorts....

And whenever we boys got hungry when the cook was off duty, we would go across the street to Rafi at his Armenian deli and eat baloney sandwiches and drink Ab-e-jo (beer or, literally, barley water).

That first night they took me after dinner through an archway into a beautiful *bagh* (garden) with a *hose* (reflecting pool) in the middle of it, and although it was dark, I could smell the incredible perfume of jasmine all around me in the air. I could hear a nightingale singing in the distance. They showed me to a wooden bed where I was to sleep, and across the garden Touss's younger brother, Kavous (as in the Kai Kavous epic), pretended to be asleep on his wooden bed throughout the entire proceeding of my arrival and my dinner because he was so desperately shy of meeting me. In the weeks that followed he quickly overcame his shyness and we became the very best of friends.

Eventually he even ventured abroad to study in Paris and became fluent in French, and I can remember at the end of each summer when he would see me to my train at Gare du Nord to head back to Orly to fly home, we would weep silently with the tears streaming down our faces as the train pulled away, him watching from the platform and me sitting glumly behind the window of my compartment. One would have thought for all the world that we were two gay lovers but we were completely innocent and crying like two brothers, as if one was staying home and one going off to war instead of to Washington D.C. to continue my studies.

Sometimes in Rome on a Sunday, without saying anything, he would pull the car over to the side of the road and the two of us would just listen silently to the eight hundred churches of the Eternal City all ringing and ringing their bells. We nicknamed Kavous Lord Halifax because everything had to be just

Photo by Khosrow Bozorgi, Agha Khan Visual Archive MIT, Bagh-e-Fin, Kashan

Photo by Khosrow Bozorgi, Agha Khan Visual Archive MIT, Bagh-e-Fin, Kashan

Photo by Zara Houskmand

so for him when it came to his attire, his cigarettes, his pressed and tailored shirts and suits, his endless perfectly polished rows of shoes...his watches, Van Cleef and Arpels...his coiffures, his eau de colognes...Francesco Smalto....

Anyway, that was my first night in Tehran, sleeping outside in the jasmine garden of summer, under a black sky thick with stars. A tabby cat suddenly came from nowhere and hopped up on my bed to spend the night purring next to my feet. I learned the next day that his name was Khrick Ali Shah (Fat King Ali) and that he had three brothers: Zard Ali Shah (Yellow King Ali), Sephid Ali Shah (White King Ali), and Motori Eshotori. The latter was translated roughly for me into Camel Motor, because he was camel colored and purred so loud he sounded like an engine. Off I went into dreamland, and everything was magic until sunrise at about five A.M. when suddenly I was violently awoken by the most god awful noise, like some kind of a steam locomotive derailed right outside our garden wall in the *kuche* (alley.) It was actually, as it turned out, a donkey, which refused to move because he was protesting his two huge saddle baskets full of Kharboseh (those Persian melons) *"Khar bos e?"* is a popular play on words: *Is the donkey a goat?* I don't think I had ever heard a donkey bray that loud, that long, and that close by before, and when one is not expecting it and has no idea what it is, it can give you quite a start!

All morning long, before the heat of the day, a stream of street vendors came drifting by calling out their wares. I was enchanted. There was even a knife and scissor sharpener and a man with what looked like a large one-stringed harp that he used to re-fluff your pillows and mattresses for hire. I came to love the sense of the passing of the seasons that these vendors brought years later when I lived in Tehran. There was a season for the red raw dates, and one for the red raw pistachio nuts, and one for those little flat tire-shaped white peaches they call donut peaches, and one for *beh* (quinces) and pomegranates, and one for *gerdou* (brine pickled walnuts). There was always something good in season and for sale in the streets, marking each season by the arrival of its own fruit or vegetable—unlike here where we can eat nectarines from Chile or greenhouse hydroponic cucumbers in the dead of winter and only the changing weather indicates the changing of the seasons or the tinsel and glitter advertising sales in the shop front windows in the super malls.

Later that first day, the cook, Roya, took me around to all the bread bakers so I could see the different kinds of flat bread: Barbari, Taftoon, Sangiak, and Lavash (listed from thickest to thinnest). I loved the way that the bakers would hang the long *noon-e-barbaris* off nails on the opened wooden doors and shutters of their shop fronts for all the world to see and smell, and I remember that one of these loaves only cost around ten cents and they were so good to eat still hot and steaming from the oven....

Next, Saburi, the former servant turned bus driver for the "Wahed Coompany," insisted I ride his bus with him for the rest of the afternoon. It was hilarious because we soon departed from his normal route and he gave me a grand tour of Tehran including Mehdune Shahyad. He only stopped the bus for cute young girls for my benefit even though most were *chadoris* (veiled.) As soon as they realized what a good time we were having, most of them joined in our conversation, and the veils gradually fell away to reveal blue jeans and western style blouses. Saboori was so proud of his bus, so proud of his city. He took me to lunch at a café at Koorosh department store, and I remember a chandelier that was several stories tall and reflecting pools and fountains inside the galleria.

What a perfect day it had been, and that night Touss's family and some of their friends took me to Hotel Darband and we went dancing. I remember that summer of 1966, the Frank Sinatra song "Strangers in the Night" was playing and so was "Hey, Mister Tambourine Man...." By the end of the evening we were all relaxed and feeling no pain and telling stories and jokes in our booth when suddenly I managed to bang my head against the large print on the wall above us. It came off its moorings and landed on all our heads.

Thank heavens it did not have a glass pane over it. Our heads went right through the paper print and there we were all within the picture frame staring at each other in utter amazement until we suddenly all started laughing. I can guarantee you that no one who was within that picture frame in Darband that night in 1966 if they are still among the quick will ever forget it. They may have forgotten my name but not that night....

Alia the Saintly man loved by all whose funeral was attended by high and low all day long.

Parvin Ansary and Vittorio De Sica

Parvin Ansary and Anna Maria Pier Angeli

Ary and Parvin

Gian Maria Volante, director of
"The Good, the Bad and the Ugly" and Parvin

Parvin and Alberto Sordi, argueably the greatest Italian comic actor

CHAPTER TWO

Berim Shomal Ba Radio Darya!

ONE DAY DURING THAT SUMMER OF 1966, WE ALL JUST DECIDED TO "*Berim shomal*" or "Go north!" as they used to say. My friend's first cousin and her Savaki (secret police) husband had been fighting again, and after giving her a black eye he came around to our house with a large smoked white fish by way of an apology but we weren't having any. We packed ourselves and her and her baby and her mom and everyone else into several cars and made a little caravan headed north. It was time to get out of the city and escape the summer heat. I recall as we headed out through a stretch of desert we disturbed a herd of one-humped dromedary camels, which took off at a trot away from us. Gradually the ground began to rise until it eventually rose quite dramatically like a great symphonic crescendo towards Mount Damavand. As we were climbing steadily, I remember shepherds selling fresh yogurt from dripping cheesecloth bundles hanging off the ends of sticks along the side of the road. It was the best *mahst* (yogurt) I ever had in my life. It added a whole new dimension to yogurt, like the way wild mushrooms taste over cultivated ones.

There were other delights in the mountains also, like tea houses and outdoor BBQ restaurants which specialized in fresh grilled trout caught in the streams there and grilled sheep's livers—and balls, too, which they called euphemistically *don balon* or sheeps tails, but they were not tails, I can assure you. We stopped at Karaj dam, and as I looked down over the precipice, the wind grabbed my cap, sending it high into the air and then down, down, down until it disappeared, just like in the song "Mio Capello" by the Italian singer Riccardo Cocciante. I remember stepping back from the edge a bit after that. As we passed under Mount Damavand, I remember craning my neck to try to look up the incredibly steep walls of the peak, which was lost in the clouds. We passed the watershed and, coming down the other side of the divide into a river valley still quite arid, I spied two storks making circles in the air below us. I'm not sure at what point the arid, bare mountains transformed suddenly into lush green forest and grassland. It was as if we rounded a bend and suddenly it was a different land. Everywhere were green, grassy knolls, large oak trees, crocuses and wild tulips on short stalks. Everywhere it was spring and things were growing, farmers planted wheat and herded fat tail sheep.

By nightfall we had made it to Bandar -e- Pahlavi to the governor's mansion, and finally I was able to meet the governor whom we had nicknamed the Grand *Goooch* (ram). Next morning he cornered me as I was coming out of the shower and grabbed my scrotum as if weighing my testes in the palm of his hand. He muttered something like "Not very big!" and then went wandering off absent mindedly. Well, I found that rather weird and intimidating. I asked my friends, his nephews, what in hell that was all about and they told me that he considered every male a potential rival in the womanizing department. Iranian men were rather like Italian men in that no matter how old, fat, short, bald, or ugly they were, no matter how rich or how poor, they considered themselves God's gift to women and if their advances were spurned, they would not feel any sense of rejection but instead would use it as just another opportunity to display their larger than life egos with statements like: "Oh well, it's your loss, not mine," directed at the latest fleeting object of their fickle desire.

On the other hand, the bright side of this attitude was that every woman was fair game to these men, regardless of their looks, size, age, income, or marital status, including motherhood, widowhood, or degree of relatedness— as in first cousins, aunts, etc. as well—so there was never any reason for a woman to feel rejected or unattractive, even if it was purely physical and not based on any desire for an *antalagh toloogh* relationship. Some young western women could not resist messing around with local men's heads. They would try hitchhiking on Khiabune Pahlavi just to create traffic jams and laugh. One American teacher went to the Caspian and fell asleep in her bikini on the beach to wake up to a humongous crowd of staring village men. I'd seen the same thing in Siena and at the Trevi Fountain in Rome, where vast crowds of country bumpkins would crowd around the summer tourist girls while they sat at little tables at outdoor cafes, just staring at them; armies, nay, nations of sexually repressed men, whose own women were kept under the lock and key of their own families. And, of course, any woman who didn't cover her head or even bared parts of her body or traveled alone unescorted by a male relative, especially a foreign, non-Moslem, had to be a hooker.

I remember once, years later, while traveling with my girlfriend from Herat to Mashad before we returned to our jobs in Tehran, we had a terrible experience there. It was a few weeks after Nowrouz (Persian New Years) and we figured the crowd would be gone. We got off the bus and hailed a taxi there and asked the driver to take us to a hotel. All the hotels were booked, but each time we inquired within, men would ask me how much I charged. Finally I came to the realization, with a sick feeling in the pit of my stomach, that these ignoramuses thought that I was a pimp and my girlfriend was a hooker. In the end we found some unfinished apartments, which the contractor was illegally renting out to the pilgrims, where we stayed. When we went to the shrine of Imam Reza and Princess Goharshad, which looked like Disney's Magic Kingdom castle, Cindy's head was veiled and we removed our shoes, but they wouldn't let us in. I said, "But we are Moslems," and they said, "It doesn't matter; you are *harejis* [foreigners]." Everywhere there were mullahs with beady, squinting, evil-looking eyes casting us furtive glances and scurrying about plotting the upcoming revolution and Khomeini's *coup d'e- tat* no doubt....

The next day we went to the train station to discover that there were no seats available at all for the foreseeable future. This was really scary, coming to the vague realization that we were stuck in what was proving to be a horrid place. Finally we found out that certain trains had some reserved cars for Iranian military and for the occasional foreign traveler who was stuck like us and so they let us on one, which was the slowest ride to Tehran imaginable. I believe this train spent as much time stopped as it did moving all the way to Tehran. It seemed like something upwards of thirty-six hours.

Anyway, back to Bandar-e-Pahlavi and the Grand Goooch. We all decided that day to transfer to the beach house, which was a great large one-story bungalow with a balcony that ran completely around its perimeter, and it was there we all ended up sleeping in the heat of the afternoons after swimming and lunch and at night with the women on one side of the porch and the men on another. Our dentist, Doctor Garagosloo, had lent us his cook, Chupan, who was a master; he would prepare and cook the birds and the fish that were the day's catch for us. It was the first and last time in my life that I have ever gone fishing with shotguns. I must say, it does have its merits. No waiting at the end of a rod and reel wondering if the fish will ever bite or if there are even any fish down there or if they like your bait or not. We went along in a speed boat looking for the tell tale signs of clusters of little circular ripples on the surface, which were the mouths of feeding schools of white fish. The skipper of the speed boat had the eye for spotting them. He would cut the throttle and we would drift up to within range and let off a blast from one of our shotguns, at which point the skipper in his swim trunks would dive overboard and retrieve the stunned fish for us—was this decadent or what? No wonder they had a revolution eventually.... And the birds, I can still see the look of terror in their big brown eyes, the wounded plovers and doves with their hearts beating a thousand times a second in my hands as I snapped their necks to put them out of their misery. I didn't shoot any of these birds, I swear. I only shot the white fish, but I must admit that, cruel

16

as it was, nothing tasted better, sweeter, or juicier than the flesh of a roasted mourning dove. It was like biting into a piece of firm ripe fruit.

No wonder the darn French and Italians would eat rows of sparrows or thrushes in baguettes, bird submarine sandwiches made from birds grilled on skewers like sparrow kebabs. I can still picture how a row of little feet would be hanging out one side of the roll and a row of beaks sticking out the other. I could never bring myself to eat one. The Northern Europeans hated the Latins for eating all their song birds as they flew over their countries during seasonal migrations. There are more shot guns per square foot in Italy than any other country on Earth. I think it has something to do with mid-life crisis and some sort of penis substitute...besides, they say that Rome is the first African city south of London!

One night I took the governor's daughter dancing—that is, a whole group of us young people and his driver and big Jeep SUV to some open-air dance floor on the beach. She had already developed a crush on me, which I found quite awkward since her rhinal development left the legendary Cyrano de Borgerac in the minor league. Her nose was just at the right level so that every time we did a slow dance, I would get poked several times in the eye. I'm not sure if my tears were from the pain or the embarrassment. Poor girl, she was definitely a candidate for the ever-popular rhinoplasty. I mean everybody was having it done, right? Shahbanou, Shohreh Aghdashlou...what the hey, no big deal. A nose job had become a status symbol among the *arrivistes* anyway.

I kept telling the band to play disco instead of slow dances, but the only thing they knew up there that summer was "Apache" and that was one beat I was at a loss to dance to. I ended up attracting quite a bit of attention because I came up with what, I thought, was a cool disco move in which I clapped one hand to the back of my neck with my elbow sticking out into the air. Turned out this closely resembled some sort of Gilan folk dance and the crowd went wild that a young American would know how....

We ended up having a pretty good time despite my occasional poke in the eye, until we got back to the governor's mansion. Goooch was waiting outside, pacing, as it was about 1 A.M., and the minute his daughter got out of the Jeep, he started slapping her about the face while she cried out professing her innocence. It was not very pretty but I later found out that the communists had placed an editorial in the local paper about the governor's daughter staying out all night dancing and drinking with foreigners.

I don't know what it was about these sisters, but they sure seemed to spend a lot of time being hit. I mean, after all we had come up here with the oldest daughter and her baby to get her away from her lunatic Savaki husband, for a break....

That was pretty much our trip to Shomal. We drove up to the border with Russia at one point and traveled along jeering in Russian at the Russian border guards from the open windows of our vehicle.

It was funny because Touss claimed to speak Russian but no Russian speakers we encountered later in Europe could ever understand him until one day in Paris, a Russian cab driver understood his dialect and he turned to me proudly and said, "You see, I told you I could speak Russian!" It turned out to be some dialect like Georgian or Chechin.

Forest Trail in Shomal

Photo by Ali Moayedian of Chalous Road.

Courtyard of Gowarshad Mosque, Mashad

Me doubling as Pietro Della Valle rowing Princess Manni during filming on the Caspian in 1975.

Photo by Martin Gray, Sacredsites.com. Princess Goharshad Shrine, Mashad

Photo by Martin Gray, Sacredsites.com. Iman Reza and Princess Goharshad Shrines, Mashad.

Photo by Martin Gray, Sacredsites.com. Princess Goharshad Shrine, Mashad.

Photo by May Farhut, Agha Khan Visual Archive MIT, Imam Reza Shrine, Mashad

Me and Cindy at Naghsh-e-Rostam

Me at Darband, 1979

Me at Bagh Eram in Shiraz

Sahar, me and the Governor without portfolio

Me and actress Atesh in film Pietro Della Valle

Sir Robert Shirley (me)

Me, Director Parvin Ansary and Assoc Director Torabnia on site at Soltanieh

Shohreh Aghdashlou and Parviz Mirhosseini on site at Soltanieh during filming of Sorab-e-Soltanieh

CHAPTER THREE

The Misadventures of Kai Kavous:
At the Chehel Setoon of Esfahan

IN THE OLD HOUSE ON KUCHE GOHARSHAD, THE ZIRZAMEEN (the basement, literally the underground) was where we had all our private parties. Sometimes it was the short cut to "San Francisco." (In the novel *My Uncle Napoleon* by Iraj Pezeshkzad, "going to San Francisco" was a euphemism for having sex.)

Sometimes we took siesta there. Often it was where Princess Nazak hid when she had evaded her bodyguards.

It was padded with Kashans and Nayeens and silk bolsters on the floor to lean against, with low coffee tables where there were bowls of fruit and cucumbers. The walls were covered with *galeems*. The lighting was subdueable. Sometimes it was almost like the ancient Greek symposiums down there. Days could go by down there without ever coming back up to the surface. There was a world in the *zirzameen*....

It was down there that a person could go to read and escape the heat of the day and the crowd...and therefore, as I write down my recollections and stories about things past, I will visualize myself seated in a pile of pillows down in the *zirzameen* writing these love notes to all my darling readers....

The first story from the basement is called:
"The Misadventures of Kai Kaous: At the Chehel Setoon of Esfahan"

It was summer of 1975 and we were filming a scene for Parvin's film *The Travels of Pietro Della Valle*. We had arrived in Esfahan a few days before by train, and there had been a lot of political intrigue within the cast and film

Princess Nazak at 17 years old.

crew over who was going to get to stay at the Shah Abbas Hotel and who wouldn't. The rest of the salt of the Earth and I didn't care, so we stayed in the less famous hotel, which was perfectly fine, while the male lead actor from Yugoslavia, whom I shall nickname Mr. Wuss, shifted quarters over to the famous hotel. Well, *la dee daaaa!*

Meanwhile I had been introduced to one of my fellow actors whom the director was trying to resuscitate, who went by the name of Manuccio from his "days at Cine Citta." Manuch was hysterical just by the absurdity of the persona he had created for himself. He adored John Wayne and had learned to walk like him and talk like him, which in Farsi is pretty funny. He kept talking about what he was going to do "after all the shotting starts!" It finally dawned on me that he meant *film shooting.* As the day for his part drew nearer and nearer, he seemed to become more and more agitated. He kept asking me and Kai Kaous how many lines he had to memorize for his part. It started to become quite apparent to us that he had been away from acting so long that he was experiencing stage fright.

I was having a few problems of my own. I was to play the part of the Englishman Sir Robert Shirley, who had historically helped modernize and equip the army of Shah Abbas and even married his daughter. My part was to take place in and around one of the ancient Armenian Christian Churches of Jolfa where we would meet Pietro Della Valle and his wife, the Syrian Princess Manni, played by the popular TV actress Atash. I was to ask them to take care of our toddler while my wife and I were going to be away from Iran for a year since I had been made the Shah's Ambassador to England. I had a magnificent costume, which along with the rest had been made by the seamstress for Roudaki Hall (The Tehran Symphony and Opera House), modeled after historically accurate etchings a Safavid scholar had provided.

My problem was that the crew had become so jealous to learn how close a friend I was to the director that they were out to get me, forever setting up little speed bumps in my progress. On the day of my "shotting," the makeup artist started acting like a stick in the mud. He kept looking at one of my eyebrows, which has one edge nearest to the bridge of my nose where the hair grows the wrong way. I mean, it is a very small part of my eyebrow, hardly noticeable, which is a pattern which actually has run in my mom's side of the family for many generations but the make-up artist kept shaking his head and looking at it in disgust and muttering, "What ever am I supposed to do with this?" You would have thought I had grown two heads. Then he kept avoiding putting make-up on my face because he insisted I didn't need any. My new contact lenses were starting to sting my eyes but I was managing to keep calm anyway.

The filming began finally. We all started out kneeling in a pew in the Armenian church, then slowly and majestically we rose and walked out into the courtyard where we came to a stop as a group, at a certain angle. I delivered my lines, which I had been handed only minutes before, and my role was done, or so I thought. Piece of cake. I loved this film acting as opposed to stage acting—no memorizing long lines, no extensive rehearsals, great!

Later, as it turned out, although my role as Sir Robert Shirley was over, my role as stunt double had only just begun. Halfway through the "shotting" of our film, Mr. Wuss, our lead actor, decided he'd had enough with sleeping in tents, the desert heat, the dust, or whatever else he felt was an unbearable hardship, and he went back to Yugoslavia. Before he left, it was discovered that he couldn't ride a horse properly at full gallop in several scenes using Shah Reza Pahlavi's horses on loan to us, nor could he row a boat on the Caspian Sea with his beloved, so yours truly—that is me, Rasool—had to do all that, pretending to be him and also filling in all the long distance shots for him after he left.

This would have been fine, but there was a scene where Atash and I walk through a beautiful forest in Shomal (The North), which is said to have famous orange birds in it although I never did see them. There is also a lake there with a mysterious castle under its surface that only emerges into the air to be seen during the dry season each year before returning under the water with the spring rains. What a fairy tale we could write about this place.

Anyway, the "shotting" went fine as I strolled regally with her up and down the gentle knolls deep in the forest with its play of sunlight and shadows. It was later, on the cutting floor back at the studio, that I got upset. Two of the editors, who did not realize that I had been doubling for Mr. Wuss, were talking to each other in big loud voices, remarking on how big Pietro's ass had suddenly gotten and how he must have been eating a lot of Celo Kebab during his stay in Iran since it was so much bigger than in the earlier scenes. I was totally pissed off but I couldn't say anything, of course. It would have only made it become a public humiliation rather than a private one....

Well, so much for me. Back to Manuch. We were supposed to shoot a scene inside the Chehel Setun itself on the second floor that night, in the music room where the niches in the ceramic walls look like musical instruments. We could not find Manuch. For over an hour we looked for him, searching high and low. Finally we noticed the light peeking out from under his bathroom door in his hotel room, but we heard no sound inside it and got no response to our knocks after trying the door, which was locked. Noticing a dripping sound we began to get worried and called the hotel housekeeping staff for a skeleton key. When we opened the door, there he was—sleeping like a baby in the bathtub with the water just about up to his nose.

When we finally woke him up and got him dressed, he started fabricating a long and complicated story about how the chef at the hotel had given him food poisoning with his chicken and he just wasn't sure if he was going to be able to act at his best for Parvin. Maybe he wasn't going to be able to act tonight because he felt so sick. Well, he got the "chicken" part of his story right anyway, and as far as that goes he was putting on quite an act as it was.

Kai Kaous and I each grabbed one side of him under each arm pit and started walking him around like those scenes you see in those documentaries about shark tanks in aquariums when the scientists have to wade around in the kiddie pool with some newly captured shark to get his circulation and breathing going again.

Finally the moment arrived for which we had all been waiting. Manuch looked majestic and tall in his light blue bejeweled costume complete with turban and feathers. He was the prime minister of Shah Abbas's court and the Shah had finally been given the green light by his astrologers that it would be okay to meet with the Pope's nephew, Pietro Della Valle, a *hareji* (foreigner.) It turns out that Manuch had only one line after walking with Pietro into the throne room and bowing before the King and presenting Pietro to him: "Your Imperial Majesty, if it pleases you, may I present Prince Pietro Della Valle, who seeks your audience..." or words to that effect.

Kai Kaous and I began snickering and finally had to run out onto the balcony of Chehel Setun where we roared with laughter, unable to further control our mirth. When we finally wiped all the tears of laughter from our eyes, we sneaked back in to find that Parvin was not satisfied with his performance and made him do it again and again and again and again...and again.... I can still remember hearing her screaming at Manuch to hold his damn feet still.

Every time Parvin yelled cut, Kai Kaous and I would run out onto the balcony and burst out laughing again. Finally, in between gasping for his breath, Kai Kaous confessed in my ear that he had switched Manuch's slippers for a pair that were several sizes too small. We were dying. The "shooting" went on for seven hours up until just about sunrise, and we lost count of how many takes Manuch had to make. Also, the power for all the cameras and camera lights, which had been brought in by long portable electric cords from some generator in the parking lot, kept failing and we were pitched into complete blackness inside Chehel Setun over and over....

What a night to remember. As the joke goes, "The only difference between this place and the *Titanic* is that they had an orchestra...."

Atash as princess Manni

Infamous walk in the woods

Me doubling for Pietro on Caspian

My big butt doubling for Pietro in forest

Pietro Della Valle

Pietro in court of Shah Abbas

Princess Manni being courted by Pietro

Princess Manni in desert

Princess Manni riding camel

Right Kai Kaous no. 1 mischief

Sir Robert Shirley and family

Sir Robert Shirley head shot

Sir Robert Shirley profile

Sir Robert Shirley's daughter

Sir Robert Shirley's wife

European portrait of Shah Abbas in collection of Hussein Davoudi

Shah Tahmasb receives Mogul Emperor Homayoun

Lotfallah Mosque, Esfahan

Modern painting by Ali Massoudi, oratory of Masjed-e-Jomeh, Esfahan

Photo by Bruno Barbey, Magnum Photos, Madar-e-Shah Mosque, Esfahan

Photo by Bruno Barbey, Magnum Photos, Shah Mosque, Esfahan

Photo by Ali Moayedian © Ali Moayedian Ali Gapu, Esfahan

Photo by Ali Moayedian © Chehel Setun, Esfahan.

Photo by Ali Moayedian © Ali Moayedian Mehdun-e-Imam, Esfahan

Photo by Ali Moayedian © Ali Moayedian detail Ali Gapu, Esfahan

Photo by Ali Moayedian © Ali Moayedian, Shah Mosque, Esfahan

Photo by Iason Athanasiadis Masjed-e-Shah detail.

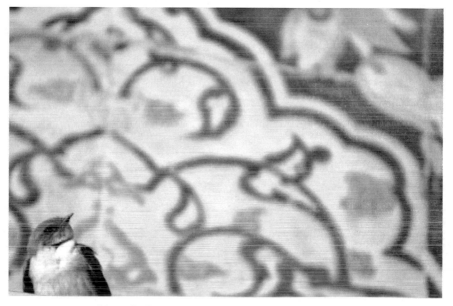

Photo by Iason Athanasiadis, Sparrow, Esfahan

Photo by Iason Athanasiadis Esfahan

Photo by Timothy Bradley Agha Khan Trust for Culture Shah Mosque, Esfahan

Photo by Kamran Adle, Agha Khan Trust for Culture,
Chehel Setoon, Esfahan

Photo by Kamran Adle, Agha Khan Trust for Culture,
Ali Gapu, Esfahan

Photo by Kamran Adle, Agha Khan Trust for Culture,
Ali Gapu, Esfahan

Photo by Kamran Adle, Agha Khan Trust for Culture,
View of Shah Mosque from Chehel Setun

Photo by Kamran Adle, Agha Khan Trust for Culture,
Ali Gapu, Esfahan

Grand Vazir

Manuch

Manucher Naderi as
Grand Vazir

Manucher the Great

Manucho and
Kai Kaous

Pietro and
Grand Vazir

CHAPTER FOUR

A Good Sport: Chehel Setun of Qazvin with Dai Jan Napolon

IN A FEW DAYS TIME, WE WERE ALL PILED ON A BUS GOING FROM Tehran to Qazvin. As soon as we were out in the countryside, the director and co-producer Doctor Parvin started to dress down the entire crew like a football coach about their lack of cooperation and professionalism and so on and so forth. I was quite impressed by the absolute silence that followed her diatribe. In fact, we rode the rest of the way in silence.

When we arrived at the Chehel Setun of Qazvin, there was a strong wind blowing in the white trunk birch trees all around the grounds of the mansion. The white trees were filled with black ravens, which were totally upset by our arrival. Seems they had very few visitors. The air was filled with the sound of them scolding us with their disapproving call: "Chalk...chalk... chalk...chalk....chalk." This cacophony of sound and wind went on for the entire time the crew was setting up, including a tower across from the second story balustrade where the cameraman could zoom in for head shots when the scene was out on the balcony. The scene had a certain beauty, in fact, with the black crows jockeying for positions on the sparse white birch branches in the heavy wind like aircraft circling a runway. The shafts and rays of sunlight came down through the flickering birch leaves and made the stain glass windows sparkle in a rainbow of colors.

I stood spellbound, watching this scene without moving for a long time, drinking in the sounds. Finally the crew had finished erecting the camera tower and, since I did not have a role in this scene, I climbed up the ladder and sat down next to the cameraman, Bijan, to watch as the scene on the balcony began to unfold. Out came an old man dressed in black velvet clothes and a lacey white collar, like a portrait of Velasquez, to meet Prince Pietro Della Valle, who had just dismounted from his winded horse with streams of froth from its mouth and bands of sweat on its flanks from a hard gallop away

60

from the field of battle where the Ottoman's had kicked our butts in Azerbaijan. Actually, come to think of it, I dismounted from the horse having played his double while he was in the party tent drinking ice water, the precious dear.…

Anyway, I was having a hard time following the dialogue with the old man screaming in Farsi with theatrically bulging eyes and shaking jowls, but Pietro was saying his lines in Italian, which I could follow better. I think Pietro was asking the old man, who turned out to be portraying the Spanish Ambassador to the Court of Shah Abbas, whether Spain would consider joining forces with the Vatican State to stop the advance of the Turks. In fact Pietro's mission in visiting Iran was to represent his uncle, the Pope, in petitioning Shah Abbas and his forces to join them, also against the Turks.

Well, the Spanish Ambassador apparently wasn't having any of it and behind him with a serious scowl on his face was Kai Kaous dressed as his page in those ridiculous pantaloons the Europeans wore back then. They ballooned with huge pleats and yet didn't even reach mid-thigh, while the rest of his legs were covered by black tights. His upper body was covered by a white baggy sleeved blouse with one of those repeating "S"curve stiff laced collars that went completely round his neck in a circle. He looked so silly it was all he could do to keep his straight face long enough to be filmed for thirty or forty seconds and no lines. But the director was not picking on him. She seemed to be focusing on trying to get the old man to stop shouting his lines so loudly and projecting his voice since he was not on stage with an audience down in the wings who needed to be sure to hear him. She kept explaining that with film acting, since there was a microphone at the end of a boom hanging right over his head but out of the sight of the camera, he had no need to be yelling, but I guess it is hard to teach an old dog new tricks.

This went on for what seemed like hours. If I had been asked who, out of all of us aspiring actors, would have been most likely to succeed, the old man would not have been my pick. However, life, with its inevitable irony, picked him, for he was Golam Hossein Nakhshinch, who went on from there to be the main star in the very popular TV series adapted from Iraj Pezeshkzad's novel *Dai Jan Napolon* (*My Uncle Napoleon*).

By evening the virus bug the crew had caught to be out to get me had spread to the cameraman whom I had assisted all day long. In what I mistook as an act of male bonding, he challenged me to a Vodka drinking contest. I should have sensed the atmosphere of a cowboy gunfight duel that began to creep into the proceeding. When I arrived at the appointed place at the appointed hour, there was a long narrow table like you would see set up with the food service for a banquet, only down the entire length of both sides ran two long thin grey lines of half pint bottles of vodka *saghi* ("doggy vodka," which is how the Persians say rot gut).

Bijan, the camerman, had kind of an odd-shaped, ungainly body. Although he was a fairly young man, his body looked middle-aged, like he had spent far too many years hunched over behind a movie camera. Tonight, however, he had the air of a champion. He exhibited a certain confident professionalism and even wore a special drinking hat for the occasion as we were outdoors in the garden of the Chehel Setun of Qazvin. I began to get the sinking feeling that he had a lot of practice at this and probably had built up a higher tolerance for alcohol in his bloodstream than I ever had.

Nonetheless, I wanted to be a good sport about it because I had the vague notion that perhaps this was an Iranian tradition and I didn't wish to offend my host by not participating—nor did I wish to be perceived as a coward. I don't think I will ever understand why so many men of every country and culture in the world seem to think it is a sign of the ultimate *machismo* to be able to ingest and metabolize vast quantities of poison and survive the experience even as the liver goes into a tailspin from overdrive, but they do. I mean, just think about it. Alcohol can be used to preserve dead fish and reptiles and other specimens of dead life for centuries in the display cases of museums....

Anyway, to make a long story short, Bijan sat on one of those office chairs with wheels and started methodically twisting the caps off of one little bottle after another, downing the contents of one after another and tossing the empties into a great tub, stopping only momentarily to make sure that I was keeping up with him. After what seemed like an interminable length of time, at which point we had consumed some obscene amount of vodka, probably near seventy of these little bottles, I suddenly realized I could no longer sit up straight let alone stand up, and I keeled over off my chair in slow motion onto the ground with a dull thud. My head suddenly felt like it was an iron anvil being struck by a hammer. I was sure that I was going to die and, frankly, would have preferred death to the way I was feeling.

Bijan's moment of self-satisfied victory was short lived, however, since every sound began to feel like someone was jabbing my brain with a knife and I began to scream accordingly. When all the cheering section finally realized that I was not joking but was really in trouble, they ended up taking me to the emergency ward of a local hospital, where I started praying out loud with the famous opening lines of the Koran: "*Bismillah al Rakhman al Rahim*," and if God had any mercy and kindness he would have snuffed me out on the spot, but instead He arranged for a couple of shots of adrenaline in my hips with giant long hypodermic needles, which returned me from the brink of my coma.

As every one of you who has been there, done that, knows, you always promise yourself and God that you will never get drunk again, but being weak mortals prone to memory loss, for some reason, given enough time, we always end up trying it again sooner or later and once again we vow it will be the last time for sure....

62

I don't know what I was thinking to have accepted the drinking challenge anyway, because come to think of it, I have never had a lot of tolerance for these foreign substances we call narcotics or stimulants. I mean, the one time I was talked into trying opium in Iran, it made me puke and everyone kept saying, "Here, eat these candies and that won't happen," but the last thing I want to do is eat something after I've puked.

One time I tried to smoke one of those little black Toscano cigars that my host in Siena, Italy, had offered me in the privacy of his dining room after a sumptuous feast. I took one puff and immediately became nauseous. I managed to avoid creating a scene long enough to be escorted to the guest room, where I was offered a bed in which to take a siesta, which by the way is a terribly civilized custom, I think. No sooner did I lie down than I tossed my cookies all over the sheets and I had only just met these people, who were in-laws of a good friend of mine. Everyone in the house was asleep, so I tippy-toed around until I found Pia, the maid, and explained the situation to her in whispers, offering her a handsome tip if she could clean the mess up without letting the hosts on to what had happened. She agreed, thank heaven.

At least she agreed to the clean up but not to keeping her mouth closed about it, apparently, because several weeks later I ran into my former host in a popular coffee bar in the middle of town and he asked me if I were ready to try one of those little black Tuscan cigars again, handing one over to me. I didn't want to appear to be rude, so I took one little puff and *bang,* I fainted dead away, landing with a crash on the floor in public this time. When I came back around, my "friend" with the cigars said: "Oh well, don't feel bad. These cigars are not for everyone. In fact, we have a saying here in Tuscany that Tuscan cigar smokers are born with one in their mouth." Ouchie, poor moms....

I wish to leave you with one more example of my intolerance for these foreign substances, which took on mythological proportions. I had just started dating my secretary at work in Tehran and I invited her to come with me to an office party being thrown by my boss, whom I had not met socially before outside the office. She met me at my house and before we went to catch a taxi to the party she offered me some hash. I said that I didn't have any cigarettes to make it into a joint with since I never smoked the stuff. So she said, "Don't worry, just eat a piece. It's much better than smoking it." Always in the spirit of not wanting to offend people who are trying to be generous to me, I obliged her. It tasted like what I imagine shit would be like...and that was that and I thought nothing more of it. We hopped a cab and arrived at the party. It was a very large house with a huge swimming pool in the side yard and lots and lots of people I didn't know.

I was having a conversation with someone when, at some point, I began to realize I couldn't remember what I had just said and had to guess what to say next, hoping it would be related to whatever I had just said. I didn't like the feeling and I worried that people would notice. That would have been bad enough, but all of the sudden the person I was speaking to's head grew very, very large and his nose, which appeared like a giant iceberg, threatened to poke me in the eye. I was terrified. It was just like that bad breath commercial they used to have on American TV.

I decided that perhaps a nice swim in the pool might sober me up. The next thing I knew, I had stripped off all but my shorts and was doing a Tarzan impersonation complete with chest pounding and yelling as I did a swan dive into the pool. Realizing at some point when I came back up to the surface that people were staring, I got a little self-conscious and got out of the pool, put my clothes back on and started looking for my secretary. I couldn't figure out why everything looked so blurry and only much later realized it was because my eyeglasses were at the bottom of the pool.

I couldn't find her so I went upstairs in this strange house and looked for a bathroom. I thought maybe I could puke that shit out of my system like you can with alcohol. The moment I shut the door to the water closet and turned around, I found myself screaming and clutching at the walls because the toilet was about one hundred miles down, appearing as a tiny white dot at the bottom of a mineshaft toward which I was falling. Horrified, I went and found a vacant bedroom and decided I would try to sleep it off. I remember realizing at some point that there was absolutely no way to stop the hallucinations, which would just have to run their course until my system had metabolized that shit out of me. It was possibly one of the most helpless feelings I have ever experienced. As I lay there on the bed, I suddenly found myself struggling through the hair on my arm, which appeared to be as big as tree trunks in a large forest, so big around I was having a hard time holding onto them.

I got up and went down stairs and tried to blend in and make small talk as calmly as I could until I noticed that my right leg was tap dancing out a tune like it was playing a drum in a rock band to some rhythm only it could hear. Finally I saw my secretary and, grabbing hold of her hand, I whispered in her ear, "I am in serious trouble. You have to get me out of here."

It was amazing because as soon as I got back to my home in familiar surroundings with no one else but her around, I became relaxed enough to almost enjoy what was left of that experience, and in fact I got an attack of the giggles imagining what I must have looked like to that crowd when I did my Tarzan impersonation.

That was the last time I ever ate shit, and that is one promise I have managed to keep. The irony was that I found out weeks later that all those people from work at that party that I was so worried about making a bad impression on were all serious *tariakis* (opium smokers) who even rubbed *looleh* (tubes of opium) on their baby's gums when they were teething. Even my ancient old landlady herself used to enjoy the *senatori* brand (the kind that was so good the senators smoked it), which I would pass on to her when well-meaning people would give it to me for Now Rouz presents...but sorry, puking just wasn't my cup of tea.

By the way, I don't mind sharing these experiences with my reading public because they should act as a deterrent and, secondly, I have no intention of ever running for public office—unless, of course, someone invites me to replace Ross Perot as the leader of the Populist Party. Sometime I must tell you what I thought about his stupid movie *On the Wings of Eagles*, about how he supposedly single-handedly went back into post-revolutionary Iran and sprung three of his arrested American employees from jail and managed to get them out of the country. I mean, for cripe's sake, anyone who was there during the revolution knows that every jail in Iran was emptied out during the revolution. His was no unique act of heroism. One guy we knew who was sent by "friends" to pick up a package at Mehrabad airport, which turned out to be two kilos of cocaine in an apparent sting operation, was in for a ten-year sentence. We used to dedicate songs to him at night on the radio. The next thing you know the revolution came and the liberators went around unlocking all the jail cells and sending the prisoners packing for home. Our friend yelled, "Long live Khomeini!" and jumped out the window of his cell onto the roof of a passing taxi which went speeding off down the street. In his wildest dreams, I'll bet he never imagined that a revolution would cut his jail sentence short after only one year. He who shall remain nameless was smart enough to figure out that the revolutionaries would probably smack him right back into jail once they figured out what he had been in for, so he left the country, passing his brother's passport off as his own.

So I'm sorry, Mr. Perot, but I'm not buying— and I guess I just told my readers what I thought of your story, didn't I?

The next chapter from *Tales from the Zirzameen* will be "How I Almost Married a Qajar Princess," or maybe how a famous Persian portrait artist showed me full length portraits of most of Iran's most famous women socialites in the nude in the privacy of his own home. Cute, huh? Each painting revealed only the head of the person until you pulled back a little drawstring velvet curtain, which revealed the rest. I was dumbfounded as to how he had talked all these women, many of whom I knew personally, into posing for him in the "all together" like that! I definitely felt a sense of reverence and awe for the man. One last joke, speaking of Qazvin: A group of Qazvinis called Mr. Bush at the White House recently and told him that they were holding Osama Bin Laden captive. They went on to say that they would be willing to negotiate a prisoner exchange if he would sent them Leonardo Di Caprio.

65

Gholam Hossein
Nakhshineh

Gholam Hossein
Nakhshineh

Gholam Hossein
Nakhshineh

Gholam Hossein
Nakhshineh

Gholam the Great

Prince, Vazir,
Ambassador

Stanco, Manucho,
Gholam Hossein

CHAPTER FIVE

The Seven Sisters

USUALLY WHEN WE HEAR ABOUT THE SEVEN SISTERS AND IRAN, we're talking about petroleum. But this time we're talking seven sisters as in *Seven Brides for Seven Brothers*. Iranians are capable of great acts of generosity, regardless of what the motivations may or may not be. Sometimes in pre-revolutionary Iran, I was reminded of the Potlatch Ceremonies I had read about once practiced by the Native Americans of the Northwest coast of North America, perhaps akin to what may have been common practice among the patrician class in the days of the ancient Roman Empire. You see, conspicuous spending on oneself, as is so common in the West, was not regarded as particularly interesting in Iran. What bestowed great social status was conspicuous spending on others.

I will start illustrating my point with a small example and then work my way up. One Persian New Years, which is the Persian "season to be jolly" and a time of gift giving, we were invited to Chez Michelle at the Tehran Hilton by Uncle Mamdahli. Uncle Mamdahli had made a fortune in the electronics retail business, I believe, but how people made their fortunes in Iran was often a mystery. He was the sort of pre-revolutionary unchastened guy who would sooner throw away a tie with a spot on it and buy a new one than take it to the cleaners.

Our dinner started with champagne and Beluga caviar by the silver bucket full to be followed by Steak-e-Paillard, but I, for one, never got that far. I had never in my life nor ever will again, God willing, become so full of caviar that I couldn't fit anything else. Besides, I had consumed so much champagne that my head was spinning and it was all I could do to stand up and find the agility to place one foot in front of the other. It was a good thing I liked caviar. Being half Norwegian, I generally like anything that smells and tastes fishy and salty anyway, including all kinds of fish roe, although some are better than others, and this was definitely the best.

We struggled back to our car and headed it down the long hill for home on Pahlavi Boulevard. It was very late at night and the streets were deserted. For a seemingly interminable while as my head swam and we had all the windows cranked down for air, we saw not a creature, not a movement, and heard not a sound other than our motor. Suddenly we came up upon the largest man I have ever seen trudging down the middle of the street in giant strides. He looked big enough to wrestle down a large bull. We were amazed and stared at him in awe as we passed him and his figure began to recede into the distance.

I had a friend named Pouran who was a divorced single mom with a little toddler daughter. She and I were just good friends and over time became like brother and sister. Surprising as this may be to many readers, I often slept over night with her and her daughter and not once did it ever occur to us that we were anything but two genderless friends. I never touched her in anyway other than brotherly, and she even arranged for me to meet another very beautiful lady friend of hers, Lily, whom she wanted me to date, another divorced single mom with a young daughter. Ironically Lily and I became great platonic friends as well, and mind you, I was dating and having sexual relationships with other women during all this time and both Lily and Pouri knew it. I had no secrets from them.

Both Pouri and Lily came from quite wealthy families. Even so, Pouri was later to risk her own life in a heroic and successful foray she made with two hired gunmen to free me from a hostage situation in which I found myself in the middle of the revolution, as I shall describe in a later chapter. I mention this here because regular civilians with no military training committed all kinds of acts of heroism during the Iranian Revolution. These deeds will largely go unnoticed by the rest of humanity other than by a few friends and relatives, but I will always owe a debt of gratitude to Pouri and will never forget her heroism, even if I'm the only one who knew for these past twenty-five years.

Sometimes Pouran would call me on the telephone at eleven o'clock at night and ask me to hop a cab at her expense to come and watch television with her and her daughter because she was lonely. I lived very far south in Tehran and she lived very far north, but it made no difference. She would wait for me even if it took forty-five minutes more to get there.

When I recommended that she take her daughter to Madrid to see Dr. Castro Viejo, the man who invented the corneal transplant, for a cataract surgery, she left me the key to her luxury apartment and car on Jordan Avenue. For a three-week period I had the use of her apartment, which was high on a hill and on the tenth floor with a view sometimes endless and occasionally above a fog bed, making it seem as if we were in an aircraft. It was right across the street from my office, to which I walked. I have never had an experience like this in any capital or large urban center of any other country. In fact, the only time I was ever alone in Tehran was when I chose to be. This is certainly a vast difference from my experience living in NYC, where after six years I knew fewer people than when I arrived and, although it had all the *bazari* (merchants) and traffic congestion aspects of Tehran, it had none of the charms or generosity except during times of crisis when New Yorkers suddenly were put back in touch with their own humanity—but it took a major crisis.

One Christmas my American employer gave each of us a frozen turkey, tins of cranberry sauce, and a box of fruitcake. My Moslem friends were always careful to be sure I was never left alone on Christian holidays or on my birthday, and I recall that on this particular Christmas, Lily invited me to bring over the turkey and trimming to her place where she had her cook prepare a sumptuous feast and even added a few British-isms like Yorkshire pudding. She didn't have to go to this trouble for me at all, but she wanted to.

The late Fari Eghbal (Esfandiary) once told me that her father would get lonely at lunch even though he was surrounded by friends and family, so he would invite over fifty friends and guests every day. The workmen in the street would smell the food cooking from the kitchen windows and the servants would run food out to them at lunchtime until finally such a long line gathered every day that they couldn't feed them all and they had to close the shutters on the windows to keep the smell of the food from escaping. She told me her father would also buy black slaves and set them free, but because they would be captured and taken back into slavery outside his estate, he would invite them to become permanent houseguests for the rest of their natural lives. Fari Khanoum didn't tell me exactly how many there were, but I had the impression that there were several dozen. She came to the sad realization during the course of our conversation that the new moneyed did not have this sense of *noblesse oblige* and the more "modern" each generation became, the stingier and less likely they were to exhibit such great acts of kindness and generosity.

It was not merely the rich who behaved this way in Iran. I can remember early on when one of my English students, an enlisted man in the Iranian Air Force, invited me to his parent's house on the weekend to have lunch. It was in the poor part of town and they had killed their last chicken in order to entertain me. When I came in the door, being careful to remove my shoes at the threshold, they immediately confronted me with a pair of flannel pajamas, which they insisted I change into to be more comfortable. I was touched. Of course, the other custom was to insist that your guests have second and third helpings even when they insist they are no longer hungry.

I am reminded of one time in Izmir, Turkey, when my taxi driver took both hands off his steering wheel to turn around and suddenly dump cologne on our heads and rub it in as an act of friendship while we went careening down the busy narrow streets. Talk about culture shock.

At any rate, one day in the fall of 1977, we were invited to a party at a garden outside of Tehran in the town of Karaj. It was a garden which belonged to the general, who was chief of all the police. As we approached the garden there was a long private roadway with cypress trees on either side leading up to the house. The trees had little twinkling lights all over them like one would expect to see at Christmas in the West. As we taxied down the lane, my friends explained to me that this party was being given by the General for a Jewish friend of his on the occasion of that gentleman's daughter's wedding. In fact this was really a wedding reception. I had never before heard of a friend paying for and hosting a wedding reception for someone else's daughter.

I had met several of the general's daughters before at the Bashgah e Shahanshahi and found them to be quite stunning and natural blondes, too, but I was not aware or prepared for the fact that he had seven grown daughters, the youngest being about seventeen years of age. They were all in a row in a receiving line as we came into the garden gate on foot after a valet had taken our car. They were so gorgeous that as I kissed each one on the cheek, I could feel myself blushing and at a loss for words...and you know me, never known to be at a loss for words. My friend told me that they were all seven from the same mother.

In the center of the garden, there was a large swimming pool featured, surrounded by melon-sized spheres made of a mosaic of colored glass cubes lit from within to make beautiful multi-colored lanterns. I was to learn later that one of the family traditions at these garden parties was for someone during the course of the night to get tossed into the pool with their clothes on. Tonight was no different, except that one of these electrified stained glass balls got knocked in along with the guest during their struggle to resist. For the life of me, why a guy would resist when three or four beautiful girls were tugging on him is beyond me, but anyway, luckily no one got hurt or electrocuted.

Two of the seven daughters escorted me around the garden since we were some of the first guests to arrive. There were five large party tents set up at various points where the fruit trees and flower beds gave way to grassy lawns. Inside these tents the ground was covered over by Persian carpets which looked Esfahani, being mostly light blue with stylized floral patterns. There were bolsters and legless divans covered with pillows and low end tables covered with bowls piled high with fruit. As the evening proceeded there were singers and musicians in some of the tents playing the daf and lutes. It was a scene from *A Thousand and One Nights*. I kept looking round for Scheherazade but she wasn't there that night—and anyway, she would have had to compete with seven beautiful sisters. I felt like I had almost died and gone to a Moslem version of paradise the night was so perfect. The guests kept arriving and the party went on into the wee hours of the night. We watched the moon rise and play in and out of a few fleeting clouds. Kai Kaous and I thought it looked like the eye of an angry dragon, but then again we were stoned at the time. We watched the moon until it began to set.

I settled into one of the tents with the live music, and we were sitting cross-legged on the carpets watching the musicians when suddenly a very attractive middle-aged brunette, probably in her early forties, sitting quite close to me could resist the sway of the melody no more. Quickly rising, she started belly dancing just a few feet in front of me. I was completely mesmerized by the impossible angle of her hips in relation to her spine at times during the dance, which looked like 90 degrees. She was almost at right angles to herself. I think my mouth was open and I was staring which drew her attention, because the next thing I knew she came right over to me and raised her leg, bent at the knee, rapidly right up one side of me then over my head and right down the other side as she spun around and danced on for awhile, only to come back and do it about five more times. By this time I must have been drooling like an idiot and near fainting from my repression. I damped my sweaty forehead with a white linen handkerchief and tried to act nonchalant. It was a good thing I didn't get up and dance with her because Kai Kaous told me later that her husband had been staring at me angrily during this whole proceeding.

As the party wore on and the dusk began to meet the dawn, the general kept coming around from tent to tent purporting to greet us, his guests, to see if we were wanting of anything, but he was actually trying to get a head count on all his daughters and their whereabouts on this magic night of nights. Apparently the things we hear about the bridesmaids and the maid of honor at our wedding receptions in the USA are also things fathers worry about in Iran. I kept thinking how he couldn't resist throwing this blow out party for his friends' daughter and, by so doing, he had brought this added worry upon himself. Can you imagine, all you fathers out there, what it would be like to keep tabs on seven beautiful daughters?

Pouran Nafisi in her early twenties.

CHAPTER SIX

The Man Who Would Be King

HOW MANY MANSIONS HATH THE KINGDOM OF HEAVEN! SOMETIMES I marveled at how many secret alleys and bi-ways and worlds within worlds, like a labyrinth, Tehran was. I could and did spend days wandering around the bazaar or around Vanak. Hidden gardens, hidden orchards, hidden museums, hidden mosques...hidden palaces, hidden clubs like the French Club right off of Mehdune Ferdowsi, *kuches* (alleys) with strange names like Kuche Bou Ali in Desashib...or beautiful names of streets like Behesht (heaven) and Bahar (spring) or Golemohammadi (rose). And always the clear water running in the *jubes* (open gutters) on each side of the street from the top of the city off the snow melt of the mountains to the bottom of the city, there to finally disappear out into the desert's quenchless sand, flushing the city clean all day and all night long, with a gentle sound of trickling water always in the background when you stopped what you were doing or saying for a moment to listen for it. This entire great city is built on a long gentle slope. It was possible at one end of town to take a cable car from a parking lot at the northern city limits right up to a ski resort or, conversely, walk right out into the desert at the other end. The economic classes followed suit with the shiny contemporary marble palaces of the newly wealthy in the north, the baroque old smoldering palaces of the old aristocracy hidden near the bazaar in midtown, and the poorest residents at the bottom of town to the south where it also got the hottest. In a desert environment, water takes on a sacred quality, hence the pool of water in the courtyard of every mosque for the pilgrims to bathe in, the *hose* (reflecting pool) in every walled garden, the water pitcher next to every toilet, and the public bathes and pre-occupation with bathing in general that Persians have. I remember my surprise the first time I saw a man blowing his nose in the sink in the running water in the men's room of a disco,

73

which turned out to be common practice. Water is associated with cleanliness, not Kleenex or T.P.

There was even a café on Takht-e-Jamshid called the Havarti Café, I believe, which had a fern grotto and waterfall inside it. You could step in out of the heat, the hustle and the bustle of traffic and noise, and there inside was this quiet secret little world. There were other magical restaurants like this as well, such as Xanadu and Serena. The latter had a big buffet set up indoors and then you carried your plate out into a fairyland of a garden with landscape lighting softly up lighting the bushes and trees and fountains quietly making it dreamlike in the moonlight with the tables and chairs sprinkled about on the grass.

In spring I can remember seeing crocuses and wild irises pushing up through the snow...or the rare treat of an early morning visit from dark brown wooly two-humped Bactrian camels sporting their winter coats, loaded with produce down from the mountains with their merchants as opposed to the usual sandy-colored, one-humped dromedaries one would see roving in wild herds in the desert. In autumn I was blessed in the afternoons by a visit from a flock of itinerant jade green Indian ring neck parrots making their rounds about the neighborhood. Arriving on the pine tree level with my patio at about the same time every day, they would raucously ransack the pinecones, pulling out the pine nuts with their long beaks, and crack them open for the meat inside.

Often I would spend all day just wandering about on foot exploring, coming across strange things like the Consulate of the Vatican City or the carpet museum, the Archeological Museum with its Lurestan bronze figurines, the Crown Jewels, and the Peacock Throne with capes made completely of seed pearls or the Kooh-e-Nur (Mountain of Light) and Darya-e-Nur (Sea of Light) diamonds, truly amazing diamonds with fitting names. I must have spent an hour looking into The Sea of Light.

Another time I found the Zur Khaneh ("power house") in south Tehran, and I had a go at the medicine clubs myself. On my first visit, at age sixteen in 1966, my friend Touss had introduced me to Ilti, who was the lightweight boxing champion of Iran. Ilti had learned to box because he had grown tired of Touss picking on him when they were kids together. I worked out that summer with Ilti at his gym and he started teaching me how to box. After the lesson, we used to walk down the street and flirt with girls right in front of their boyfriends without consequence because they all knew who Ilti was.

Now that I was living in Tehran in 1974, I started studying Kung Fu and Tai Kwan Do with an Iranian Air Force lieutenant, Ali Akbar, whose avocation was martial arts. His little house in an obscure part of town was mysterious. From the moment you stepped inside, you were in China. A little birdcage with rice finches softly tweeting caught your attention first and Chinese music quietly played in the background somewhere, and there was Ali doing Tai Chi out in his little courtyard in a black Chinese suit of clothes with red frogging. It was so unexpected. As my eyes adjusted to this shadow world I could see Chinese wall hangings with their characteristic tall hills and peaks and mist dwarfing the tiny huts and tiny mule team in the foreground, trying to put man in his proper place in the scheme of nature and the universe.

Society life in Tehran had a dreamlike mirage effect. I found myself drifting into private parties with live entertainers. One day prince Kamran Pahlavi wandered into one at the apartment of the daughter-in-law of the Ambassador to Rome, who was my friend Touss's cousin by marriage. Kamran was handsome and reserved, and the only thing I remember is that he drove a Ferrari and he used to play with Touss when they were little children. Another time I found myself at a private wedding of another of Touss's cousin's, Mohsen, in the large garden of a mansion belonging to the owner of a large private bank called Chemical and Industrial Bank. I remember his bride was named Ziba and she had one sister married to a Greek and another married to an Italian, as if there were some status associated with marrying foreigners. During the course of the evening I started talking to another cousin, who turned out to be Princess Niloufar Dowlatshahi, half sister of Princess Nazak and daughter of Hamid, brother of the Shah, considered the black sheep and not allowed to use the Pahlavi name. She was charming, soft spoken, and extremely intelligent, idealistic, and well educated. She had studied structural anthropology with Claude Levi Strauss and it was her life goal to help preserve the Iranian nomadic culture of the Qashqais, Bakhtiars, and so on. Since I had a degree in anthropology myself, we had a learned discussion as the wedding party; vapid ode to the nouveau riche proceeded. That I had casual access to the highest levels of society, denied to me in my own country, was part of the paradoxical experience of my life in Tehran.

One day, I somehow found in Tajreesh a *khanegah* (house of worship) of Sufis who welcomed me and my girlfriend with open arms. As we entered into the mosque, an old man sitting in the entryway pressed money into our hands. This was the first and only time I have ever been given money for going into a house of worship rather than having to part with it. The women, unveiled, would sit on the floor on one side of the prayer hall and the men would sit on the floor on the other, but we were within sight of each other and I never felt such a sense of brother and sisterhood as I did there.

One day I discovered the Golestan Palace, another day the Negarestan Museum filled with miniature portraits of Qajar princes and princesses who looked exactly like their present-day descendants: the family I was getting to know who were the pretenders to the former throne.

The first time I had been to Tehran when I was sixteen, I had paid a visit to my friend's cousin's palace in an old part of town near the bazaar. The little back alleys were too small to drive a car through and the narrow little door way belied the splendor hidden within. Once inside there was a beautiful garden with real Greek and Roman statues surrounding a long rectangular fountain with a little moss covered island in the middle from which issued a jet of water. In the reflecting pool a small wood duck completely golden in color swam about. We were greeted by three white Pyrenees dogs on the way into the house, and once inside I was shown what looked like colorful Persian carpets framed behind glass on the walls of the salon. Upon closer inspection it turned out to be carpet-like patterns made up completely of matching butterflies, which Dadush's father and four uncles had collected from all around the world. I had never beheld anything like this before or again. And last but not least, that day I was introduced to a cool summer drink made of blenderized Persian melon and crushed ice.

This was my first encounter with the former royal dynasty. There were tall Lombardy poplars bordering the gardens, shimmering silver to green in the breeze, and one could hear the cooing of doves. The servants told me a fable that these were thought to be some sort of sacred mourning doves, which had no feet and spent their entire lives in flight.

As time went by living in Tehran, I used to go to another of their family palaces, their aunt's, also in the old part south of the bazaar. Again, the winding alleys and an obscure little door opened onto a beautiful garden. One side of the living room was a half circle colonnade two stories tall and open to the garden. If there was a way to close it off from the outdoors in winter, I couldn't see it. A long narrow reflecting pool ran like a stream through the living room out into the garden and it had little jets of water staggered along its length making tiny arches into it, similar to the Genat Al Halifeh in Granada or the Taj Mahal. I had never seen a private residence like this. The son was quite an accomplished martial artist. I believe he was a fifth degree black belt. One day at a cocktail party in this room filled with porcelain and china and cut crystal wine glasses and decanters and crystal chandeliers, he put on a display with Nu Cha Ku sticks, one set in each hand, whirring them about for all the world like in a Bruce Lee movie without so much as hitting anything in the room. I held my breath in disbelief.

We use to play rummy and backgammon there and sometimes our rummy games would last all night and so we would have dinner and stay for breakfast, too, especially after the curfew had started. I would usually end up sitting out the rest of the game in no time flat since even the opening bets were more than I could afford, plus they played tavli (backgammon) faster than I could count. I had to content myself just watching and eating fruits and cucumbers and *pesteh* (pistachios).

As we became better and better friends, I would sometimes be invited over by myself. I can recall one night sitting out in the garden on the patio under the moonlight being served tea by three Qajar princesses, the mother and her two daughters. It was quite amazing really. The old servants and retainers had been with the family so long that they were too doddering almost to walk let alone serve tea and so there we were in the dusk, what a picture, three princesses serving little old me and also serving their own aged servants tea.

I also met Uncle Hassan before he died. He was a fine artist and his house was filled with his paintings, mostly of landscapes and still lifes, and he was teaching art at Tehran University at that time.

As the years went by my adopted Persian family decided I should marry into their cousin's family and they went about getting me engaged to the older sister when it was the younger sister I secretly admired. The man who would be king was extremely happy in his marriage, which, it turned out, my adopted family had helped to arrange decades before, so out of appreciation he offered the use of one of his palaces in Vanak for our formal debut. I remember that night; my family made me shave off my moustache and I had already converted to Islam. They got me all dressed up and then off we went in a limo to Vanak. This palace was more modern than those of his siblings and it was all white travertine marble with square columns and blue domes and an Olympic-size swimming pool and cypress trees. We met him and his family and I shook everyone's hands and kissed cheeks and gave my rehearsed honorifics. Then, just like in the movies, his niece and I were allowed to walk together through the garden with the entire family following at a discreet distance.

During the months that followed, the two sisters threw a nice party for us at the Chiminey discotec, and my betrothed took me by herself to see Sylvie Vartan in live concert with her dance troop at the Hilton.

This family was so gentile, so kind, so wealthy, so famous, and so well loved—and they wanted me. I just couldn't believe it was really happening. This family had a mystique about them that even protected them during the revolution. They were completely left alone by the revolutionaries and none of their assets were attached.

To make a long story short, I never went through with the arranged marriage because I wasn't romantically in love with my betrothed. As an American unaccustomed to arranged marriages, I just couldn't get myself to go through with it. I didn't think it was the right thing to do and so the dye was cast and I, with my high ideals, condemned myself to a much more mundane life as a wage slave for eternity until death do us part.

Every day we make decisions that effect the rest of our lives, but most of the time we do so unknowingly. This one I made while completely conscious with my eyes wide open.

To make an end of this tale, I will tell you of the last time I saw the man who would be king. It was the opening day of the new cable car system built by Batman Batmanian at the north end of town, which in two stages allowed one to park one's car in the lot at the base of the mountains and take a ride all the way up to the ski slopes.

It was spring and the air was very festive. Many people had been invited out to the open and had packed picnic lunches. We got off at the end of the first cable car ride, which ended in a gorgeous meadowland filled with little low growing white daisies and chamomile. As we walked about we suddenly ran into the Pretender there with his liveried valet, both dressed in white lab coats. The valet had a long butterfly net and was skipping about after Lepidoptera. They were genuinely glad to see me, and His Would-Be Majesty spent some time explaining to me about the different species and which ones they were trying to catch. They handed me a butterfly net and told me to have a go at it.

After quite some time I became totally frustrated because the butterflies were so fast up there I couldn't catch any. Finally a great black and white speckled long horned beetle flew slowly by and, not wanting to return completely empty handed, I easily bagged it.

His Would-Be Majesty explained to me that different species of butterflies lived at different altitudes and flew at different speeds and that it was no small wonder that I was having trouble here because the species we were after was one of the fastest flyers there was. He laughed when he saw the long horned beetle and actually knew the scientific name for it. He took the beetle from me and said he would add it to his collection as something to remember me by and I was shyly flattered. That was the last time I ever saw this magnificent man.

P.S. How many of you remember the old lady dressed in red from head to toe who used to go sit in a doorway on the northeast side of Medune Ferdowsi every day? I was told, according to urban legend, that she had been doing this for the past nineteen years because her lover had been drafted into the army or had to go away for some such reason and was not sure when he would be free to return, so she had promised to wait for him there every day at Medune Ferdowsi, dressed in red so he could spot her right away.

Girl in trance, women dervishes in Sanandaj,
photo by Aryana Farshad copyright 2003

Photo by Iason Athanasiadis, women dervishes in Tehran

Photo by Iason Athanasiadis, men dervishes in Sanadaj

Darya-e-Noor (sea of light) diamond, National Jewels Collection, Tehran

The Kiani Crown of Qajar Dynasty Fath Ali Shah,
National Jewels Collection, Tehran

My Namzad at a Polynesian party when she was ten.

Crossing Mehdun-e-Ferdowsi

Flowers

How we normally saw her in Ferdowsi Square

In Medhun-e-Ferdowsi

In traffic on way to her bench

On way to bench

Lady in Red

Resting on her bench

CHAPTER SEVEN

My Friend Touss, The Grand Master of Sobriquets

MY FRIEND TOUSS HAD A NICKNAME FOR EVERYONE HE LIKED AS well as one for those he didn't much like. It was mostly for endearment. Sometimes the nicknames were less than flattering but in good fun...for the most part. It usually had to do with someone's habits, appearance, or an expression they used.

It all started when we were in boarding school together in Rome. Later we formed a student club called U.L.F., which was our Swedish friend's first name. We said it stood for United League of Free Thinkers. Touss nicknamed himself Der Fuehrer, and I was the Red Baron, which was shortened to Baron, and sometimes Touss just called me Shander, as in Alexander the Great, because that devil burned down Persepolis in all its glory and grandeur. His brother Kavous was Lord Halifax because he was so mannered and meticulous in his dress, especially shirts and ties, his tobacco, his cologne, his shoes—one would have thought he was the Prince of Wales himself.

We had a friend purported to be very well endowed, i.e. well hung, and his name was Iraj, so his nickname became Eeejpistol or Eejquipment. Then there was Touss's cousin Hot Lips and his cousin Dadush, which was already a nickname from his real name, Mohammad, whom we nicknamed Slow, as in slow motion. In Rome we had a school friend named Ronny who couldn't pronounce *roots* with his cockney accent. He would say "Voots" so his nickname became Voots. We had another friend nicknamed Bozee, which I never understood except that we were all jealous of his Lancia Beta Zagato. Funny, I never knew his real name until about twenty-five years later when I happened upon him quite by chance in the streets of New York City and he handed me his card: "William Preston," it read. I never would have guessed in a million years.

School days were chock full of nicknames. There was Boozone, whose real name was Fourio Valbonese. He prided himself in being quite a ladies' man so we nicknamed him Boozone, which is Italian slang for a gay blade to whittle him down to size. Poor man, whenever he was with us and was to be introduced to someone new he would rush through his name as fast as he could to beat us from introducing him as Boozone, but the faster he spit out his real name the less comprehensible it became and so we would still succeed in introducing him as Boozone. The poor man developed a complex. We then shortened Boozone to Biuze, which became "On account of the buse!" There was J.C., because he always said "Jesus Christ" with a Brooklyn accent. I think his real name was Richard Young. Kyra was nicknamed Smilie. There was Bwoston, nicknamed after her Bostonian accent. Jean Rossi was Poor, and he used to always talk about "Le 'D.S.' du mon pere...," his dad's car, which we thought was funny because it sounded like "Deesse" or his dad's goddess....

There was the nuclear physicist named Bahram whom we nicknamed Eeeereeesle because he was very obsequious and when he squinted looked rather like a weasel. We loved him though. He had a thick German accent when speaking English because he had studied in Germany; he sounded like Henry Kissinger. He used to say: "Shhhpeeed Shtimolates!" Sometimes we called him Jack Sharkey because of his overbite. The man was brilliant and drove the biggest BMW they make and his wife was bright and beautiful, and yet with our sobriquets we cut him and everyone else down to size. I'm not sure who the hell we thought we were exactly, but "Aaah, the arrogance of youth...."

There was Houshang, whom we nicknamed Phenomen, as in phenomena because he was so clever in business and popular with beautiful women, etc. There was Farokh, whom we nicknamed Sayed Mobarak due to his solici-tousness and fondling over friendship; he could never do enough for you. There was Roya, the maid we nicknamed Unicorn, or Cornonaaz, because of her well-defined nose. Her toddler son we nicknamed Bache Guatre because he had goiters until we got them fixed. There was Amu Ansary, whom we nicknamed Amu-I-am-so-sorry-I-am-so-sorry, and there was Khosrow, whom we nicknamed The Finance Minister. Amu Sepabad we nicknamed Goooch, the Ram, due to his philandering.

The old waiter at the French Club in Tehran we nicknamed Lopti, as in Le petit, because his French was atrocious but he was very, very *simpatico* and really tried extraordinarily hard to please the guests.

We created our own planet peopled by our own cast of characters, and it made life more interesting, more personal and more intimate. There was Lee Marvin Gay, The Pike, Mr. Bishop, Dutch, Tector and Lyle and Angel and Mapache, and the entire cast of Sam Peckinpah's *Wild Bunch* whose names we assigned to each other and our friends.

Long before *Rocky Horror Show* we started a fan club for the *Wild Bunch!* Dozens of school boys who had never seen the movie knew all the lines by heart thanks to us. "Get those horses up!" "How does it feel, Mr. Harrigan, to do your share of the killing, with the laws arms around you?" "Good!" "You dirty son of a bitch!" "If you two boys don't like equal shares then why in the hell don't you just take all of it?" "Silver rings your butt, them's washers!" "We'll join 'em!" "The Temperance Union?" "Kiss my sister's black cat's ass!" "Hell, I should have been running whores instead of stealing army horses!" "While Angel dreams of love, Mapache eats the mango!" "Hell will be waiting for us!" "I wouldn't have it any other way!" "Me neither, Pike." "Hell, they wouldn't look in their own back yard!" "What makes you so sure?" "Being sure is my business!" "We've got to start looking beyond our guns...those days are closing fast!" "Maybe a payroll, maybe a bank...." "Boys, I want you to meet my fiance!" "Your Excellency, with your permission, I need a bath!" "With my permission you all need a bath!" "It won't be like it used to be...but it will do!" "When you side with a man, you stick to him...otherwise you are like some kind of an animal...you're finished, we're finished...all of us!" "But he gave his word!" "So!" "Well, it was his word!" "It's who you give it to!" "Mr. Thornton, Mr. Thornton, you rode with the Pike, what kind of a man are we up against?" "The best! He never got caught!" "Finish it, Mr. Bishop!" "And I suppose we should give him a proper burial complete with a choir and a church supper!" "What's in Agua Verde?" "Mexicans, what else!" "I happen to know that eqvipment is issued only to U.S.Army personnel?!" "Believe me, we share no sentiment with our government!" "How can you stand it so hot?"

I will never forget these lines, nor will the rest of the fan club, after thirty-seven years. You can imagine how hilarious it was to hear and see two young Persian brothers and me reciting and acting out all these cowboy movie lines. Sometimes when *The Wild Bunch* came to town at revival theatres in Paris, especially if it was the director's special uncut version, we would rent out the entire theatre for our crowd and kids who were seeing the film for the first time from our group would be shouting out the lines right before they were spoken in the movie. It was awesome— yes, it was childish, but it was our childhood, after all, and it made our ordinary lives more interesting, and for that I will always thank my good friend Touss.

Touss was such a film aficionado that he knew the names of every character, no matter how minor, in Hollywood films from the '30s, '40s, and '50s. It was truly amazing. Characters who otherwise might have gone unnamed in my consciousness into eternity, he immortalized for me...actors like Gabby Hayes, actors whose nameless faces you instantly recognize from a hundred stand-ins for decades, extras in cowboy movies like Slim Pickins or Johnny Ireland or the perennial G.I.s in war films, he knew all their names. He also knew, by the way, the names of every U.S. Congressmen and Senator, which put me to shame.

He knew more about the workings of the U.S. Government than I did or ever will. He also loved the rock stars like Barry White and Sir Elton John. Touss loved the English language. I helped him learn it in sixth grade in 1962 when he arrived from Persia speaking not a word, and he came to spout many Shakespeare quotes and biblical quotes like, "The Phillistines are ubiquitous!" He loved Edgar Allen Poe and could recite by heart, "Helen, thy beauty art to me, like those Nicene barks of yore, that o'r the perfumed sea, the weary way worn warrior bore to his native shore...Helen thy beauty art to me like the glory that was Greece and the grandeur that was Rome...."

The women loved Touss and Kavous, too. They were lined up to see them. I was always like the acidulated intellectual eunuch, the U.N. observer as it were, the critic, bearing witness to it all like a court historian, a chronicler but always on the side lines or in the dug out waiting it out. I mean, the girls liked me well enough, but I was much more of a monogamist than a polygamist, usually dating only one at a time. I didn't have the charisma, the animal magnetism, the charm, the looks, the panache, the style, the aura of wealth and power of these two earnest young men. I was always at Touss's side, his *aide de camp* as it were, and I came to be known by some as his Malajak. We would take vacations together to Samos, Greece, on summer breaks from college. When we parted at holidays' end, I would often for days afterwards see an illusion of him talking to me in my own reflection in the windows of trains or airplanes in the darkness of night. It was eerie.

That is all over, long over...twenty-seven years ago now. It died with the revolution, just one more casualty on the diaspora's long list. Somehow, somewhere our childhood—like in Peter Pan—vanished, our friendship died, fell through a crack in the universe, a black hole, a twilight zone, a hole in my karma, and lives only in my recollections. I never imagined that could ever happen at the time. I'm not sure how or why such things happen but as Hafez wrote, "The world is like a whore, it can love you and give you many gifts and you can love it back, but it will never be true to you in the end...."

Notre Dame International "Roman Way" yearbook, 1966

NDI Yearbook School Dance, 1966

Me in school play, "Lucifer at Large" NDI Yearbook, 1966.

Zurkhaneh (Strength House) men with medicine clubs

CHAPTER EIGHT

The Incredible Doctor G

ONE OF MY RESPONSIBILITIES WHILE WORKING FOR BELL HELICOPTER IN 1978-79 was to handle the disposition of the human remains of any employee who died in country in Iran. I was amazed to discover the amount of docu mentation required when someone dies abroad, and during the year I worked for Bell I became a bit of an expert; out of the approximately nine thousand employees and dependants who worked there, ten of them died under my watch. Bless their hearts—or souls, I should say! According to the mysterious Doctor G., Coroner General of Tehran, they all died of infarctus. No matter their age or gender or weight or other obvious contributions to their demise such as alcohol or drugs, fractured skulls from automobile wrecks, or bullet holes, it was infarctus. I mean, I suppose in a sense he was correct because when ya' die, eventually your heart does stop ticking but...anyway, I am get- ting ahead of myself.

One time I had literally just gotten off the plane from escorting an em- ployee back to Detroit who required a surgery to re break and reset his leg— which is a story in itself since I went along because we were short of nurses and no one thought to tell me, and I didn't figure it out until after the plane left Mehrabad Airport, that he was also withdrawing from heroin. Anyway, no sooner had I gotten off the plane having successfully discharged my duties and arrived back at my office, when my boss, without a word of greeting, sud- denly lay down on the floor with his hands crossed over his chest and his eyes closed in a pantomime of a stiff. Someone whispered in my ear that the next of kin, a son and a husband, were waiting in my office for instructions. A poor lady in her forties had actually died of a heart attack this time, while sitting at her kitchen table, right in front of her teenage son who watched helplessly, having been unable to successfully call for an ambulance because he couldn't speak any Farsi. Unbelievable!

I was right in the middle of explaining about what arrangements and flights I would make for them to accompany her casket back to their hometown in the USA when one of my associates who didn't know they were in my office leaned his head around the corner and shouted out at me. "If you don't hurry it up, that stiff is going to walk to the morgue all by itself!" Talk about mortified. I died a little death right then, and if the floor could have opened up under me like in *The Return of Topper,* I would have gladly jumped into the abyss. The father and son and I went right on talking as if we had not even heard the remark because we were too stunned to acknowledge it.

So let the games begin! A trip to the Tehran City Morgue was always an adventure, and besides, it was right near the Zur Khaneh, where I would go watch when I was done at the morgue and sometimes work out with the wrestlers with their stone medicine clubs to the beat of a tambour and a chant.

The first step in the process was to take the passport of the deceased to the American Consulate, where the Consul General would cancel it with a great big inked CANCELLED stamp. That in itself was a bit weird, but you see a dead person can't have a valid passport even if its date hasn't expired yet. Next the Consulate would issue you a Death Certificate in triplicate, which certified that the deceased was really dead, which you need to collect life insurance, get them in and out of the morgue and air cargo, and many other things.

Once all the paperwork is in order, filling the equivalent of a large three-ring binder, you head for the hospital to collect the corpse in a body bag and usually also a small bag with personal effects, like his watch, wallet, rings, toothbrush, and so on, for which you need to sign a receipt—you know, things a next of kin might want. Then you wheel the stiff on a gurney to the back of your parked station wagon in the parking lot and haul it into the car. Then you drive to the bottom of the town, which during the revolution could get pretty hairy. In fact one time, I had two stiffs in the back of the station wagon and ran right into a motorized column of the Iranian Army crossing in front of where I needed to go, which was also under siege from the revolutionaries, and bullets started flying all about. It was at that time that I decided that the only one in the car who would be upset if he caught a stray bullet would be me. My fellow passengers wouldn't mind because they already looked pretty dead. I backed out of there and left the vehicle, stiffs and all, in the parking lot of our HQ building until the next day when the fighting had died down. What's one more day in the sun anyway?

My biggest fear had been that, if two employees died at once, they might get mixed up during transit and arrive at the wrong funeral back in the good ol' USA, and here I was with two stiffs. Oh my God! Finally on Friday, which was the Moslem Sabbath, I made it to the morgue with my charges. It was closed. There were all kinds of stiffs not even in bags just hanging out all around the floor of the lobby waiting for the offices to open up again on Saturday (their Monday). I remember quite vividly a young mother side by side

Photo donated by Jahangir Golestan-Parast of his father's Zurkhaneh in Esfahan in the 1950's

Photo by Bruno Barbey, Magnum Photos, Zurkhaneh

with her baby. They didn't even have ID tags wired to their big toes. No one from the coroner's office had seen them yet. The custodian, the same one who had finally let us in, had been opening the door all night long to take in the day's catch now strewn about the floor. I remember there were a lot of boys who looked like street urchins, bicycle messengers, newspaper boys not even in their teens, but he refused to touch them because he was superstitious and so he watched as I slung one of my charges over my shoulder and asked him to open up a chute they used to slide the deceased down into the morgue after hours. I sent the first one down the chute and he got stuck part way so I had to go inside and haul him the rest of the way down. Then I went back for the second one and repeated the same procedure, struggling under the weight while the doorman just watched blankly.

I imagine not many of you have had an opportunity to work with stiffs. The world of morticians is another one of those secret worlds we all know exist but try to ignore. Anyway, if you have ever tried to move a bag of wet cement, that is like trying to move a stiff. They flop the wrong way every time you try to lift or move them and they are "dead weight," yet they are soft and subject to bruising and damage just as they were when they were alive so you must exercise great caution while you struggle with them. The only good thing about working with stiffs is that they don't talk back to you.

The next step in the process was to go out and buy a set of new clothes for the stiff appropriate for a funeral so when the casket was opened back home "Stateside" they would look sharp. If it was a guy, I would buy them a white shirt heavily starched, a basic black suit if they didn't own one, and a black tie, black socks and no shoes, since generally open caskets had a split lid which allowed the half from the waist up to open separately from the waist down portion so viewers would not normally see the feet. If the deceased were a woman, clothes shopping for her, just as in life, was more complicated.

After about a week I would get a call from Doctor G's office that my stiffs were ready for pick up and the autopsy reports were done. And of course it was always infarctus, even if the deceased was twenty-five years old with a big knife wound. Doctor G always looked quite pallid and wan. His skin had no color to it as it rarely was exposed to sunlight. He even had a little gnome of an assistant for all the world like Igor, complete with a limp, a hunchback, and one eye swollen shut which he would squint at you from with his head curiously cocked to one side like a bird of prey or a vulture. If this had been a movie set I can't think of any two actors more perfect for this scene. Doctor G would send Igor to get me a demitasse of espresso that smelled like formaldehyde and invariably, after thanking them profusely, I would pour the coffee into the pot of a large rubber tree plant he had in his office the moment they weren't looking. Then Doctor G would promenade through the refrigerated warehouse with me slightly behind him while he obliquely glanced at me from time to time with his peripheral vision to see if I was freaking out yet.

This was also my cue, when it was just the two of us, to slip an envelope into his lab coat pocket with about $250 cash in it, without which the same process would mysteriously take two or three weeks longer. He would not say a word about it, but as we kept walking he would pat his coat pocket with his hand contentedly.

I shall try to describe what this frozen world looked like. It was almost like a sculpture garden. There were narrow aisles between neat rows of gurneys with the dead on them like a view inside Sleeping Beauty's castle, as if a spell had put everyone into a big sleep. Some of them were in strange poses, not necessarily lying down flat. From the big toe of every dead man, woman, and child was an ID tag wired to it like a luggage tag. Doctor G would walk me to where he thought my customer was, and then I would open his cancelled passport to the photo page. We would roll him over on his back if necessary and then I would sometimes have to wipe the frost off his face with my coat sleeve before holding the passport photo next to his face to get a positive ID. Once that was done, Igor would wheel in an aluminum casket alongside and we would wrestle the stiff into it, give his clothes and hair a final once over, and then call the ambulance driver to back up to the loading dock.

Then the fun would begin. I would ride shotgun next to the ambulance driver while he would always take advantage of his vehicle and his siren to go like 100 miles an hour and push cars off the side of the road or go up on the sidewalk to get around traffic jams and act for all the world like we were trying to get a heart attack patient to the emergency ward, and he also managed to hit every bump and every pot hole along the way. It was useless to protest. By the time we would get to the air cargo terminal at Mehrabad, I would climb down out of the ambulance hunched over like an arthritic with a case of kidney stones. One time when we got to the air cargo terminal we found that a car was parked right in the middle of the entrance, making it impossible to get to their loading dock, and in this instance we didn't have a lot of time to spare until the flight. Besides, we were reaching the limit as far as lack of refrigeration could go. There was always some kind of black humor associated with these proceedings reminiscent of Mark Twain's Limburger Cheese story. I got out of the ambulance and hailed a small cluster of pedestrians who were idly standing around chatting to see if the car belonged to one of them and it did not. I explained my predicament and then talked four of these guys into helping me lift the car out of the way.

No matter what difficulties surrounded the final disposition of the remains of a Bell Helicopter deceased, it was still always far easier to send out one of their employees in a box in the cargo hold than it was to send them out live (deport them) in the passenger compartment of the airplane.

To illustrate my point, one day my employee relations counterpart from Bell Helicopter in Esfahan called me to ask me if I could assist him early the next morning at the airport. He had been given the assignment of escorting an employee back to the USA because they wanted to make sure he got to his destination. This poor soul had only been in Iran for a few weeks. Apparently he came with some serious mental problems that obviously had not just developed overnight but which had not been detected in the screening of the hiring process. I didn't like the sounds of that much. "What exactly do you want me to do, Dennis?" I inquired. "Just be there with me between the two flights to help me restrain him if it becomes necessary," he replied. I liked the sounds of that even less, but Dennis forced me to take pity on him since he was going to have to babysit the guy on the entire sixteen hour plane ride. I brought my driver, Hakim Mohammad, a devout Moslem, with me as a back up.

I shall never forget this incident, particularly since I happened to know that the individual's name meant "freedom" in one of the Slavic languages. He was of slight build with sandy-colored hair with a crew cut military style, and he was a man of very few words. He was young, and he seemed quite calm enough as he walked between us into the terminal. The moment we got inside he bolted. He ran as fast as a damn jackrabbit into the crowd. It was like he had been shot from a cannon in the circus, but the incredible thing was that he was not trying to escape. He suddenly reappeared on the luggage conveyor belts running back and forth excitedly on them as if he were a child playing on an escalator. Dennis, my driver, and I gave each other a knowing look and approached an accessible portion of the luggage belt cautiously and waited for his approach. The moment he was within range, I whispered, "One, two, three!" and we gave him a flying football tackle, bumping him off the conveyor and down onto the floor. God knows what the travelers around us thought of this activity. Dennis then forced the last two tranquilizers down the guy's throat and sent Hakim and I out to find a twenty-four-hour pharmacy to get a refill on what was obviously a controlled substance. Furthermore he told us that we only had about an hour before the effects of this last dose would start to wear off. By some Iranian-style miracle, we came back in time with a big bottle of the right stuff with fifteen minutes to spare, and we waited around until we saw the two of them board the plane. I never heard anything more about Mr. Freedom so I guess Dennis kept him successfully tranked-out for the entire ride.

Sometimes employees would disappear for days on end, never calling in or reporting, and it would be my job to locate them. One time a helicopter mechanic had come up from Esfahan on a temporary assignment and never showed up for work. I was asked to go to his hotel and investigate. According to the front desk at the Tehran Intercontinental Hotel, he had checked in three days before but had never left his key at the desk or been seen since. I took the elevator to his floor and walked to his room and began pounding on the door and calling him to no avail. Finally, I got housekeeping to open his door for me with a passkey so I could investigate for some clue that might lead to his whereabouts.

The very first thing I could see from the open doorway was a pair of bare legs hanging off the end of the bed. He was completely comatose and would not respond to any stimulus I could think of, including a bucket of water. I searched and searched the room, under the bed and in the medicine cabinet in the bathroom, for some evidence of what kind of substance he had abused but could find nothing. Finally I opened the sliding door of the clothes closet and on the carpeting beneath his clothes, which hung neatly on hangers, was a neat row of empty fifths of Scotch whiskey, Absolute Vodka, Bombay Gin, Beef Eaters, and bourbon, and I was beginning to wonder if he could have possibly survived all that. Just then the telephone on the night table rang, startling hell out of me. I picked it up and my boss's boss asked if I had located the gentleman in question yet. I said I had but that he was not talking at the moment. The boss then angrily insisted that I give the phone to the employee. I said to no avail that the man was unconscious but the boss wasn't going to take no for an answer, so I held the phone to the ear of the unconscious man for a few minutes while the big boss chatted him up. After a few minutes I got back on the phone and he finally got the picture and told me to find a way of getting him to the detox center at the US Army hospital uptown. I located a hotel nurse and elicited her assistance. She couldn't have been more than five feet tall, but she was wiry, strong, and sharp as a pistol. She arrived at the room with a wheelchair with a tall back, and the two of us essentially lifted him into the chair and strapped him into it with cargo belts of some kind. Everything was going smoothly and we had managed to get him into the elevator and across the lobby still unconscious without attracting too much attention from all the hotel guests and dinner guests who were milling about. Then just as we were entering the revolving front door he came to with a scream and stuck his arms and legs out, preventing the door from rotating with all three of us stuck inside it.

By some miracle and the combined adrenaline of the little nurse and me, we hauled him into the back seat of my car and had him lying prone on the back seat with the two of us sitting on him while Hakim peeled rubber out of the carport, heading for the detox center. The Armenian hotel nurse had even had the presence of mind to put on the baby locks of the car doors. Once I got him into a padded cell I had to stand watch in there with him until his immediate supervisor got there. At one point he sat up and seized a plastic bottle of liquid soap and started to drink it, so I had to do another flying tackle and wrestle it out of his hands. He was a big son of a bitch too. Once his supervisor arrived I watched in amazement as the supervisor started talking military talk to this former military person, who suddenly became compliant and meek as a lamb with nothing but "Yes, Sir" and "No Sir"! My mission accomplished, I got the heck out of there and went to one of those public baths where I paid a scrubber to wash me with boiling hot soap and water and brushes before I went home. I remember the scrubber looking at me reluc-

Intercontinental Hotel now Laleh Hotel

tantly and gingerly asking me if I were a Moslem before he would scrub me. I pointed to my equipment and said: "Of course I'm a Moslem, can't you see I'm cut!" He gave a great show of relief and then good-naturedly began vigorously scrubbing and singing softly as he worked. Of course the scrubber had no way of knowing that practically all Americans are circumcised because they are so squeamish about hygiene, so I had been cut when I was a little baby far too young to protest.

Anyway, the point of all this is that, on the whole, it was far easier to deal with dead employees of Bell Helicopter than live ones, Doctor G. not withstanding!

As the great actor comedian W.C. Fields had etched on his headstone:" On the hole, it is better here than in Philadelphia!"

As a footnote, lest you think I am morbid and insensitive, my group became so good at this process of dealing with the disposition of the human remains of American employees in Iran that other companies and foreign nationals came to us for consultation and advice. I never had any emotional problems dealing with death and with informing and assisting the next of kin until, one day after the revolution had begun, I got a phone call from two Venezuelan girls who were in tears and hysterics. I had become friends of theirs when I was still working as an English teacher at the Neeru Havaii (Air Force) where they also were teaching. When they calmed down enough to become coherent, I found out that their third roommate and childhood friend from the same town in Venezuela, a quite tall and attractive girl both in personality and in appearance named Mabel, had been struck down and killed the night before when she and her boyfriend were leaving a restaurant by a speeding vehicle of someone trying to get home before the martial law curfew began.

For the first time after dealing with ten dead strangers, I was confronted with the death of someone I knew personally and liked. Finally I was overcome with normal grief commensurate to what the occasion demanded and I found myself unable to give them advice. I put them on hold for a minute and explained the situation to my friend and co-worker Charlie who took over and handled their situation like a prince. God bless him!

101

CHAPTER NINE

The Gathering Clouds in the Summer of 1978

ONE DAY I HEARD ON THE NEWS THAT BANK WINDOWS IN TABRIZ were being smashed by Islamic fundamentalists. How was it possible that they were getting away with that, I wondered, since the Shah had a 400,000-man standing army? Was he losing his grip? I never and still don't understand how a strict Islamic bank can make money without charging interest. How does that work? Do they loan money for free?

I went to my neighborhood branch of Bank Sadarat and had the manager wire transfer all my money to the USA. I remember Mr. Sedeghi laughing at me and saying: "What are you afraid of? Nothing is going to happen here." A few months later that branch was burned down.

I remember two years earlier, on our way to work at Mehrabad in the employee bus, one day some Savakis in plain clothes, wearing jeans in fact, but waving Uzis and wearing light blue army helmets signaled to our driver to pull the bus over to the side of the road. They told us to dismount from the bus and walk the rest of the way into the base.

Once we got inside the air force base, there was complete bedlam. All the civilian neighbors had come inside the base to escape the imminent fighting and the cadets were wandering around in a disorganized manner without any apparent commanders or plan.

Across the street from the base, the secret police had surrounded a building and then called in a helicopter, which promptly dropped a napalm bomb on the roof and then rocketed a parked car. No prisoners were taken and no questions were asked. A group of plotting revolutionaries in one of the apartments within the building had just been taken out. We, the witnesses of this horrific event, had no one to complain to. At the time I had no interest in politics per say and had never even heard of Amnesty International, where I could have reported such an event.

In such a beautiful country and culture I had been blinded from the plight of a lot of very unhappy people. I could not fathom that we were on the eve of a revolution. It was the quiet before the storm. Some people knew it and could see it coming, but not me. The former ambassador to London, who had been the youngest ambassador in modern Iranian history when he had been appointed ambassador to India, committed suicide. He had a gambling problem and over a four-day period had lost several million USD at a casino in London. The foreign ministry refused to cover his gambling debts. His father refused to bail him out again, and finally even my friend the president of Bank-e-Sadarat refused to make him a loan, and so he had taken his own life in the end rather than face and live with financial bankruptcy and disgrace. I loved his daughter; she was so sweet and bright and her husband was so not. I remember her weeping at the Bashga-he Shahanshahi (The Imperial Country Club) the day we got the news; it was the only time I ever saw her husband smiling. I wanted to deck him. For me this individual event became symbolic of the self-immolation and suicidal course that the corrupt leadership in general was embarked upon. Like an implosion, it was rotting from within.

At any rate, the excesses and abuses of the regime were starting to make it unravel, come apart, rip at the seams, corrode from within. My Italian friend Sandra, visiting me from Tuscany, saw it coming and told me it was coming as we sat sunbathing poolside at the Shah Abbas Hotel in Esfahan, until a busload of Japanese businessmen arrived in suits and noisily took the place over. She could see all the discontent. I had grown acclimatized to it and couldn't see the forest for the trees.

Some of the swindling that had gone on was particularly spectacular. The same trainloads of government-subsidized sugar were sent back and forth across the border, collecting the same subsidy over and over. Volumes could be written about all the get-rich-quick schemes that actually were pulled off. Trainloads of cement were lined up at the borders when there was enough sand in Iran to make all the cement in the world.

The Shah had become more and more of a recluse, substituting a life-sized cardboard cut out of himself in his limo for the annual parade commemorating the victory in Azerbaijan.

One day as I was walking home along Meydan-e-Ferdowsi, I saw a police car pull over a lone driver for speeding. Two policemen got out of their car and went over to the driver, who emerged from his vehicle looking huge as he stood upright. They spoke for a few moments and then, the next thing I knew, the driver was beating hell out of both the cops at once and I stepped out into the street to walk around the disturbance. I remember thinking to myself that this was not a good sign.

Another time near Khiabun-e-Shah Reza, I saw a man running down the sidewalk with a young policeman in hot pursuit. The fugitive arrived at a phone booth and started running around it in circles with the cop behind him. A small crowd gathered in a greater circle around the scene and began jeering the policeman. At some point he lost it and started viciously head butting members of the crowd in their faces with his helmet. This gave the fugitive his chance to slip away. I had never seen anything like that before where a crowd had helped obstruct "justice." The police were definitely beginning to show signs of their inability to control the subjects.

It was not long after this that fighting began in earnest and the martial law authority imposed nightly curfews in all the major cities in Iran. Night after night began a great outcrying of human voices shouting death to the king. I wonder how he felt listening to that great united voice ringing the air like a plague of seventeen-year locusts, sitting in Niavaran Palace wondering when the mob was going to storm it.

One evening I was with my friend Pouran, leaving her beautiful apartment tower, the Dumas, on our way to dinner at the Imperial Country Club, Bashga-he-Shahanshahi, when in the lobby I received a page from the receptionist that I was wanted on the phone. I couldn't imagine who knew I was there but it smelled like trouble, especially since I had forgotten that it was Ashura, the holiest Shiite religious holiday of the year. It was Bahram, one of my assistants, telling me an unbelievable story. Evidently one of our illustrious Bell Helicopter employees had gotten totally drunk on this the holiest day of the Shiite calendar year and weaved down the hill in his car hitting every parked vehicle, ricocheting back and forth from one side of the street to the other all the way down to the bottom of the hill, where he had crashed. A U.S. embassy official who happened to live at the bottom of that hill offered him refuge, and in the meanwhile an angry crowd of the owners of the damaged cars had gathered outside this house and were threatening to burn it down unless the employee came out and paid for all the damages.

I politely listened until Bahram had finished recounting his tale and then I posed the inevitable question: "And just what, exactly, am I supposed to do about it? Go out there and try to tell this mob of irate owners carrying torches to break it up and go home?"

"Yes!"

"Oh," said I. "Me and whose army?"

Bahram says, "Well, Security seems to think this is an employee relations function?"

"Oh they do, do they? Does anyone know you are having this conversation with me right now?"

"Yes. All the security officers are standing around listening as we speak!"

"Bahram, you are a consummate ass! Furthermore, you work for me, not for the Security Department, and they have no business giving you direction. Since you seem to be under their management, kindly convey to them my profound belief that this situation calls for the intervention of the Iranian Martial Law Authority—not little old me. Goodbye!"

I then proceeded on my date and had a great dinner at the Club with the pleasant company of my friend. The head waiter and the bartender were two Lebanese brothers who had left Beirut in order to avoid the fighting there. They were very sophisticated and pleasant and we use to give them French designer silk ties for Christmas since they were Christian. I shall never forget several months after the revolution was complete, we returned to an all but abandoned country club to actually see a pack of feral dogs running around the golf course pissing on the greens and snarling over scraps in the sand traps. When we got to the club house and went to the dining room, we found the two Lebanese brothers in their tuxedos standing, one behind a bar with no alcohol on its shelves and the other at the waiter station standing watch over an empty dining hall. It was a sad picture, and I began to recollect how many pleasant times I had spent with so many friends there in better days.

Anyway, on this night, I dropped Pouran back at her place and had the taxi keep going to take me home, where I went to bed forthright and had a good night's rest until at about seven A.M. The phone rang and it was the third in command of Bell Helicopter himself, the former US Army General S. He spoke to me in a voice full of irony. "I understand that you were insubordinate last night?"

I replied, "With all due respect, sir, I do not take orders from the Security Department nor was it in my job description to face down angry mobs single handedly without the assistance of riot police. Frankly, you may take my job if you insist that this is an area of my responsibility because risking my life to save some sorry ass, culturally insensitive ignoramus was not part of the job description when I signed on for this gig!"

The next day, my boss was demoted and a former military-type, all-American good old boy was put in on top of him. Within one week, his house was bombed and he was on the next plane home, and our original positions were restored plus a combat pay bonus. A few months later when we were busy evacuating thousands of people from revolutionary Iran, the same general had me stop everything I was doing to track down a traveling cage for his wife's dog that she wanted to put on the plane with them on their way home.

I don't know whatever happened to the Ashura drunkard!

Then one night right after Khomeini had started making short wave radio broadcasts from the safety of Paris encouraging people to violate the curfew and get shot to die as martyrs for Islam, a horrible thing happened—at least as horrific as Bloody Sunday in January of 1905 in St. Petersburg when Tsarist troops opened fire on peaceful demonstrators or Tiananmen Square, but the world has forgotten the ten year "Silent War" between Iraq and Iran in which millions of people were killed and the USA armed and encouraged Saddam Hossein to start and sustain war on Iran because he was a CIA appointee and Americans are sore losers who don't like getting kicked out of countries where they have oil concessions, so why should I expect anyone other than Iranians to know about or remember Black Friday? How many nameless people died in the Silent War or were left orphans or quadriplegic while the rest of the world only knew one Iraqi name: Saddam Hossein, which is still the case, and only one Iranian name: Khomeini? An Austrian doctor, Doctor Bueller, who had operated on and reconstructed the bones of my best friend's leg when he had cancer, voluntarily went to Iran after the war to help fit out all the amputees with prostheses.

On this particular Friday night, in September I believe, I was at home because the curfew had started when I began to hear the shouting of voices perhaps seven or eight city blocks away. They were not the rooftop, "Death to the King" shouts; they were different. I called my long time school buddy who lived on Behesht and Bahar, Jim, and asked him if he could hear the shouting. He said he could. I asked him if there was a soccer game going on at the sports stadium near his house and he said no. Then we began to hear the automatic gunfire. It sounded like hands clapping and the shouting began to turn to screams and sobs and wailing with great tremulousness and fear. It was bloodcurdling and much of it was female voices, and I remember thinking that the Shah was even stupider and more indifferent to the suffering of his people than I had suspected if his men were mowing down unarmed men, women, and children in peaceful protest of his regime. How many Americans are clueless? In the Boston Massacre of 1776, only one person was killed and it was a long time ago. I remember the shooting, the crying, and the screaming went on and on and on and on from nine P.M. to two A.M. when it finally stopped. Five hours of shooting, and I bet they were bullets either made in American or Russian. I was weeping, by myself upstairs in my apartment, lying on the cold terrazzo floor vomiting and crying.

The next day, the top management of Bell Helicopter called us into a meeting and told us that something had happened last night but had any of us actually seen anyone get shot? They extolled the virtues of keeping calm and not spreading rumors. I choked on my rage...and reminded them that there was a curfew so of course none of us had seen the event. I mean, talk about a self-serving case of denial.

People were just so out of touch with reality, it was amazing to witness. One day there was a bomb scare in our office on Jordan Avenue. The "Pie Man" had just come by so Joanne, one of our travel agents, who had bought a big pie from him, suddenly bolted from our group huddled together out in the parking lot while the bomb squad went up on the roof to run back inside to fetch her pie.

As I recounted in the last chapter, Mabel, my Venezuelan friend, had been struck dead while leaving a restaurant with her Iranian boyfriend by a speeding hit and run driver who was trying to get home before the martial law curfew began. Her two roommates from the same home village, Isabel and Maria, had called me weeping and crying to ask for advice on what to do

106

about getting the remains sent back home to Venezuela because they knew I had dealt with the deaths of Bell Helicopter employees and dependants in the past. As I mentioned, I was amazed to discover that when it was not impersonal but someone with whom I had actually been friends, I found myself almost powerless to do anything and so I had asked one of my co-workers, Charlie, who didn't know them, if he wouldn't mind explaining to them the steps involved in getting the death certificate and autopsy from the city morgue, getting the passport cancelled at the appropriate embassy, and making arrangements for air freight with whichever airlines could take it to Venezuela and then paying the ambulance driver at the morgue to transport it to the air cargo terminal, notifying the next of kin by telex or phone and informing them of what time to meet the casket on the other end. It was an elaborate process which was daunting even in times of peace when there wasn't a revolution going on with air traffic controllers on strike and pitched battles blocking the streets. They thanked me and that was the last I ever heard of them. They had been three such innocent and friendly girls, who had on several occasions invited us over to their apartment for dinner parties in which they offered us their national drink, called "Matte," which tasted like rotten grass and I never did acquire any taste for it. I imagined how devastated her family and friends would be when they got the news and how brave she and her two childhood girl friends must have been to leave their little town in Venezuela to come over to Iran to teach English at the Imperial Iranian Air Force Language School and how they must have been admired for it back home. And now Mabel was coming home in a box and Iran was in chaos.

The buttons were beginning to pop off and fly from the shirt of the Iranian Corpus as its chest began to fill with breath like a sleeping giant finally waking up—to revolution!

The petroleum industry workers went on strike and there were people lined up for days trying to buy kerosene for their space heater *bokhharis*. At night or on the Friday Sabbath you could see ropes tethering all the jerry cans together in a line on the sidewalk unattended so that their owners wouldn't lose their place in line the next business day.

There were lines of many city blocks of vehicles waiting to buy gasoline from the few service stations to be found that were still open with petrol to sell. One day two Bell Helicopter employees were in a taxi that got out of the slow lane jammed with waiting cars to go around them, when suddenly a bullet went right through the windshield and into the cab driver's head, splattering blood and glass on them. Apparently a soldier had mistaken the taxi driver's move for an attempt to cut in line and so he had used his rifle to put a stop to it. There were lots of weeping people involved in this one, including the young and inexperienced trigger-happy soldier who wept the most of all.

Bell Helicopter eventually started circulating a newsletter every day to report incidents that had happened the night before in an attempt to keep us informed. As a result, while Bell was still bringing in plane loads of new employees up until two weeks before the Shah finally left, there were also thousands of employees and their dependants quitting and leaving at their own expense rather than wait for Bell to finally offer an evacuation program. I remember at one point being assigned as a "meeter greeter" to meet a plane load of Bell Helicopter recruits and dependants "right off the boat," mechanics from little towns in East Texas. I'll never forget they were all wearing yellow Bell Helicopter baseball hats as they had been instructed to do and I was wearing my navy polyester blazer with a Bell patch on the front pocket and the gray polyester pants, the standard employee relations dress code, which I had been ordered to do. The very first thing I did was order them to whip off those yellow hats. I can remember them freaking out as our bus bounced down crowded streets with gun battles going on and bullets flying and them wondering why the hell they had come before they had even reached the "Commodore" Hotel.

Meanwhile as the Iranian world was falling apart with ever increasing momentum like the ice pack breaking up at the South Pole in spring, life went on and I was having an office romance. I had spied a Persian girl at work one day I had not seen there before and I fell in love with her face, especially one day when I saw her at the drinking fountain with her lips pursed round the jet of water. I fell in love with her soft full lips. Her name meant a dream and I was dreaming about how much I wanted to date her. My American girlfriend had returned to the USA many months before the revolution had begun upon the completion of her teaching contract and I was a bachelor again and on the prowl.

I can't remember exactly how it happened, but I have a vague recollection that one day I offered her a ride home with my car and driver and me and on the way invited her to stop and have dinner at the Tehran Hyatt Hotel with me before we took her home. To my amazement and delight, she accepted. From that day on we started dating, and although we were very discrete at work, my driver apparently couldn't keep his mouth shut because some of our Iranian employees would make remarks to her when no one was around, like, "What's the matter, aren't Iranian men good enough for you?"

Weekends she got in the habit of having her aunt drop her within a few blocks of my house on the pretext that she wanted to visit a girlfriend and then instead walked to my house. I would anxiously wait for the doorbell to ring, knowing it would be her, and there was a tremendous air of excitement when she would come in, silhouetting my doorway, slightly out of breath and flushed. Shutting the door behind her, she would throw back her chador off her shoulders and we would kiss. She had taken to wearing chadors when the revolution was coming to life in order to keep a low profile. One day she told me that she had found an artistic picture she had once had taken of herself for her now ex-husband of herself sitting on her bed with her bare back turned towards the camera and she wanted me to have that photo. That weekend she arrived at my house quite upset because her male cousin who had been with them in her aunt's car, had found the photo and unwrapped it. When his mom had parked the car and gone into a shop to buy barbari bread, he had turned to my dream and said to her that he would keep the photo and put it over his bed. She was angry and sickened by this little pig but could not protest as her aunt would have guessed that she was en route to give it to some man and in Iran divorced women were even more sheltered by their families than were virgins. To this day, twenty-one years later, I long for that picture or at least a glimpse of it.

In my mind's eye I can still see a scene worthy of the Doctor Zhivago movie, when the six-mile long march was in full swing half a block south of my house and my girl arrived at my door in a white lace chador like a divine angel with the sunlight behind her. She dropped her veils and I carried her up my stairs and we proceeded to make some incredible love all the while to the sounds of the army of protest marchers outside my house on Shah Reza Avenue. I remember thinking how affronted the fanatics would have been and how we probably would have been stoned to death had we been caught in the act...which had the effect of heightening our excitement. It was very romantic, don't you think? Of course the revolutionaries were very romantic too. I remember watching the march and seeing Volkswagen vans driving up and down the lines offering hot meals to the protesters for free, many of which were driven by engineers and other professionals. It was the dawn of the short lived Iranian spring, and what a feeling of solidarity and brotherhood and sisterhood there was. The day that Shah Reza left, millions of people took to dancing in the streets. They bent their windshield wipers outward and tied white ribbons in increments to them and then turned on the wipers so the white ribbons waved back and forth festively. People were singing and rejoicing and I took to dancing with them, too, and I was there the day Khomeini arrived and the city was completely deserted like a ghost town, not a creature stirred, not even a dog or cat. The proletariat had gone out to the airport to see him arrive. They didn't know what they were in for with that lunatic with his thick stormy black eyebrows whose sinister visage seemed anything but religious, more like criminally insane, yet even though Black Friday should have been a warning of things to come, his ends justified his means. He even eventually prosecuted a true saint, Ayatollah Taleghani, who had once been forced to watch his own daughter being raped by Savak agents. Each day in the paper the tabloids would have black and white photos of the naked bodies riddled with bullet holes of the officials of the Shah's regime who had been executed the night before, many of whom were my friends, like Doctor Said Said, speaker of the Tehran City Council, or my employer like General Khosrodad. It was like the Reign of Terror after the French Revolution, except instead of a woman instigator of the executions it was this old priest. The revolutionaries were so frightened that to spare any of the former regime might risk their returning to power, they were out for blood. Poor Hoveida; Khomeini's son awoke him at four A.M. and shot him in the head after stating his accusations as "Sins against heaven and earth...." Hoveida, whom I had met personally one summer when I was sixteen visiting Tehran, at a reception in the garden of the Foreign Ministry held in honor of all the Iranian college students studying abroad on government scholarships who were home for the holidays. Hoveida, who had personally called to wish my best friend well when it was discovered that he had bone cancer. Like a cancer, Iran was killing its own intelligentsia, its best and its brightest, and those brains who could escape did, often in spectacularly daring ways like the former chancellor of Tehran University Nahavandi who dressed like a woman in chador (and he was a big man) and rode in the back of a van across the border into Pakistan or other famous persons like Manoucher Farmanfarmaian, who walked into Turkey.

Americans lead such sheltered lives. They are eons apart from the realities of the people they bomb and I am praying that they don't bomb the cradle of Western Civilization again. At the time I first wrote this, the second bombardment of Iraq by the imperial son of the imperial father had not yet taken place. Now all we hear protested is the 2000 American dead in a war the US administration started. None of the media, to my knowledge, have offered any statistics on how many Iraqis have been killed so far in this latest Bush adventure. The bombing and invasion of Afghanistan after 9/11, a country already devastated by ten years of massive Soviet bombing, was the first time in the history of the USA that it had started a war—and who even remembers it started bombing Afghanistan October 8, 2001? "The War on Terror" is a cliché for war on dissidents. I am not surprised that finally a few senators are wondering if he should be impeached for authorizing spying on American citizens in the US without a warrant.

It is inconceivable to me that during the Silent War Scud missiles from Iraq were actually careening down the streets of Tehran. It is unimaginable to me—and yet everyone remembers—the V2 attacks by the Nazis on London during WWII with their characteristic whistling dive bombing sound as their fuel became spent, stalling their rocket engines in flight to send them into free fall descent, raining death and destruction and terror. Why is it that the victors can be so sensitive to their own suffering but not so to that of the vanquished or to their victims when we all share our humanity in common? How many times have I heard Afghans say that an Afghan life is worth nothing in Afghanistan? How did that come about in a country so full of innocence and beauty and devotion to God and loving kindness which I experienced in 1977, and how did Iranians who are the most generous and tolerant culture on Earth come to be portrayed as the bogeyman of the Western world? My universe has been turned on its head, my dear friends.

All you victims, you refugees, you diaspora, my heart hurts with you. I see in my mind's eye a recollection of the pistachio tree, so full of nails that you couldn't see the bark, dead without a leaf in the courtyard of the tomb of Timur in Herat, and with it died the hopes of all the barren Afghan women who had placed those nails there in the hopes that it would make them fertile...so they could mother new life, new humanity, and new hope.

Photo by Patrick Chauvel, Sygma Corbis Photos, Mile Long Protest March

Unknown photographer, Black Friday Massacre

Photo by Michael Setboun, Corbis Photos. Funeral at Behesht-e-Zahra after Jaleh Square Massacre

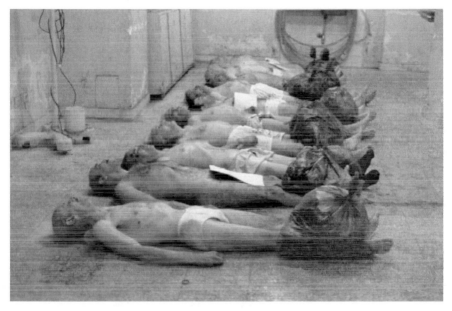

Photo by Abbas, Magnum Photos, Death Reigns

Photo by Patrick Chauvel, Sygma Corbis Photos, Shah's Imperial Guard attack civilians

CHAPTER TEN

The End of Camelot

EVERY NIGHT THERE WAS SHOUTING FROM THE ROOFTOPS OF "DEATH to the King," from the throats of millions of unhappy people. Every day there were reports from Bell Helicopter H.Q. of shooting incidents and riots and curfew violations from the night before and who was on strike that week: the air traffic controllers, the petroleum workers, the gas stations. We were a country falling apart like the breaking up of the Antarctic ice pack in the spring thaw. Millions of megawatts of suppressed hostility were coming to life.

Bell employees were leaving voluntarily in droves even as new hires were still arriving. The Shah was becoming more and more reclusive. One day I found myself alone in the VIP lounge at Mehrabad Airport on the second floor. I used to hang out there between meeting and greeting Bell Helicopter employees arriving or leaving the airport. It turned out that the entire airport had been cordoned off from the public, and as I peeked down from the blinds of the VIP lounge windows, there right below me not more than a few yards from me I espied an Air Iberia jet liner land and taxi up to the apron. The door opened and down the stairs came King Juan Carlos of Spain to be met by the Shah of Iran at the bottom of the stairs.

The two grimly reviewed a row of Niavaran palace special guards, "The Immortals," as they were called. I couldn't help wondering what the point was. Little did I know that the Shah was looking to Spain as a model while contemplating how to retain himself as monarch and at the same time give his country a democracy in a situation in some ways similar to General Franco stepping down and restoring Juan Carlos to the throne.

From my vantage point in the window of the VIP lounge, I was glad I was not one of the revolutionaries who wanted the Shah dead because if he were more than five or six yards from me I'd be surprised. Not knowing his mind, it appeared to me as if, like in the story of *The Little Prince*, the two monarchs were off on their own asteroid, divorced from everything else in the universe and the whirring and buzzing of revolutionary activity around them. It was as if they believed that somehow, by reviewing troops and playing tin soldiers, the order of their universe would be maintained.

Similarly, as fewer and fewer of my compatriots remained in Iran, I found myself partying with the US Embassy staff after hours for lack of anyone else with whom to play. The consul general at that time was Barbara Belsito, and there was Tom Farrell and Cy Richardson, who were commercial attaches I believe. At any rate, I remember one night we were having a cocktail party in one of their apartments while shooting was going on in the streets outside. I tried to express my concern for what was happening to Iran and only managed to draw cynical commentary out of the partying officials: "These people are only getting what they deserve!" or "You think this is something, you should have seen the revolution in Haiti. I could barely hide behind trees in the garden to narrowly avoid being hit by bullets..." and so on. For them it was just another occasion for a war story, as if it were long over already and not still happening right outside our window. There was a surreal air about the juxtaposition. I felt thoroughly disgusted, made polite excuses, and walked home sticking to the shadows and expecting a soldier to yell: "East!" (halt) at any moment.

My beloved adoptive country was falling apart. As the process began to gain momentum, I was working in headquarters one day up on Avenue Jordan when we were radioed by the martial law authority that the curfew starting time had been lowered to six P.M. from nine P.M., and since my apartment was way south by Avenue Shah Reza, I decided to stay over night at H.Q. I ended up staying in that building for a week without ever leaving, there was so much fighting going on by then. Finally I decided I would chance making a run for home to get a change of underwear and socks and maybe even a shower. One of our managers started complaining out loud that if I went home that I would not be coming back and he didn't want to get stuck having to do all the work by himself. We had spent the whole week shredding photographs of Bell top managers posing with the Shah and other generals from the Shah's armed forces, among other things.

I snagged a taxi, and as we drove across town I noticed lots of rallies going on at every street corner. At one traffic light where we were stopped someone in the crowd shouted, "Yankee, go home!" By the time I got to my apartment down by Shah Reza, I saw that there was a large armored truck blocking the entrance to my alley, Kuche Khagani. It had a heavy machine gun mounted on a tri-pod on the back of it and three soldiers were sitting back there smoking cigarettes. I said hello and explained that I lived at the back of the alley and as I passed around them I asked them what they were up to. They explained that a rally was going on at the teacher's college across the street. Amazingly enough I had never before noticed the teacher's college right across the street from my house. I offered them tea but they acted annoyed and declined.

The very moment I got to the top of my stairs and shut the door to my apartment, they started shooting their machine gun. Good grief! I called back my office and tried to explain to the supervisor that I would not be able to return until the shooting stopped. He whined like a baby. "I knew you were going to do this and leave me stuck here all by myself." I told him to wait a minute and opened my kitchen window and held the phone receiver out the window so he could hear the shooting a few yards down below. That calmed him down.

When I eventually saw him again a week later, he humbly confessed that, the day I had gone home, that night the headquarters building had been under siege and he had been forced to lie down flat in a bathtub in one of the executive bathrooms to avoid being hit by the ricocheting bullets around the office suite. He was a very large man well over six feet tall so it must have been quite a feat. I imagine his knees must have been sticking up and at risk....

Meanwhile once back inside my apartment I found that in my weeklong absence, my two Persian carpets had been removed by some relatives of my karate instructor, Lieutenant Rudbari, because I hadn't paid for them yet and they needed the money for some relative in the hospital. Master Rudbari had bought his way out of a lifetime contract in the Shah's Air Force with $9,000 that he had raised by selling everything and anything he had and had long since departed the country before the revolution had begun. I had heard he started a karate school in L.A. but I never found him again years later when I Googled him except for the last known address of an apartment he had once lived in there. When friends disappear on me, it leaves me with a feeling of unquiet. He had been a real friend and teacher to me, straightforward, honest, and dignified despite his simple background. He had the profile of a golden eagle and a great deal of poise. He taught me Kung Fu and Tai Kwan Do in a little courtyard in his tiny three-room house in a poor neighborhood. All the décor was Chinese, as was his *ghee* and slippers, and in stepping from the brawling traffic ridden noisy streets of Tehran into his little microcosm of China, complete with soft Chinese music in the back ground as he did Tai Chi, it was almost surreal, like Alice stepping through the looking glass.

Back in my apartment I also found, to my dismay, that my landlady, assuming I wasn't coming back, had thrown all my personal effects into the vacant lot next door, which people used for trash in general. There were something like twelve thousand dollars worth of receipts for money Bell Helicopter owed me for various expenses I had incurred on their behalf blowing around out there, so once the shooting stopped I spent the better part of that afternoon rounding them up and rummaging through piles of debris.

Quite oblivious to the pains she had caused me, my old Kurdish landlady kept weeping over a picture of one of my former British roommates whom she kept saying that she would never see again. I hadn't seen any evidence until now that she had ever taken much notice of him and I personally had no strong liking for him myself, especially the way he had ingratiated his way into Bell Helicopter by making an end run around me to my boss right toward the end. I got even later by getting him shipped out on one of the first evacuation flights, but now I am getting ahead of myself. I got tired of his endless weeping and complaining about his girl, Millie, who had dumped him. As far as I could tell from the only time I met her, which was also to ship her out of Iran, she looked like a little tramp, but they say love is blind.

Anyway my Kurdish landlady, who used to smoke opium with me, kept weeping and saying that now that Khomeini was coming everything was going to "*Khoob mishe!*" (Get better!) and I soberly told her that I seriously doubted that: "*Khoob nemishe!*" (Won't get better!)

A few days later I got a call from security about a man named Tommy Lawrence, who was in Tehran Hospital and scheduled to have liver surgery within two days. He wanted back to the USA for that. The idea of having major surgery made him nervous in the middle of all this fighting and strikes and power failures, even if they had their own generators. Now here was a request for an assist that I could get behind. I went that very night with my driver over there to his ward and asked the duty nurse if we could visit him. He was very nervous when we found him alone in a private room and adamant about not wanting the surgery done here. I calmed him down and shut the door and told him to get dressed. I went back to the nursing station and asked her what it would take to get the patient released from the hospital. That would take a note from his doctor, who would not be on duty until tomorrow.

I thought on my feet for a New York minute and then I asked her if I could see the patient's records. As soon as she turned her back and started looking through the file cabinet, I skipped back into Tommy's room with my driver and, supporting him on each side under the arm pit, we quickly and quietly swept him out of his room, past the nursing station, and into the open elevator. The second we got him into my car we made a bee line for Mehrabad airport and I called security on my walkie talkie: "Pappa Two, this is Pappa Four, mission accomplished. Can you meet us at the departure lobby? Over!"

"Pappa Four, this is Pappa Two, I copy. Roger that. I will try to get him on Pan Am standby. Call me the minute you get to the terminal. Over!"

"Pappa Two, this is Pappa Four, I read you, over and out!"

I loved talking on the radio because I could play act all the clichés I'd heard all my life on TV and in movies. (The only hitch was that whoever else had a walkie talkie within Bell Helicopter was on the same wave length, so occasionally one of the head honchos would bust into my conversation to tell me to belay something he felt was a security risk to be discussing over the air waves, which needless to say I found embarrassing.)

I then explained to Tommy that what we were going to attempt was very iffy, that the airport had become a maelstrom, a madhouse of a million Iranians climbing over each other and riding on luggage conveyor belts trying to get to the head of the line, trying to get to the ticket counters, trying to get the hell out! If we didn't manage to get him on standby using medical emergency as an excuse then I would arrange a place for him to spend the night until we could get him out, hopefully the next morning when most all the westbound flights left anyway. Once we rendezvoused with the security wonk, I told Tommy he was in good hands and that if anyone could get him on standby, Mr. Gonzales was the man. I also told Gonzales that if he needed any more help to call me on the radio. Gonzales, by the way, looked a lot like Sonny Bono. Tommy smiled faintly at me and disappeared with Gonzales into the crowd. I noticed out of the corner of my eye riding above the crowd a middle-aged Persian man pushing a baby carriage almost nonchalantly along on the luggage conveyor belt headed toward the Pan Am ticket counter.

My man Hamid and I went and had a tea up on the observation deck before heading for home and I went and purchased a bottle of cognac out of the duty free shop where I still had friends. I figured that since I was spending the night alone I still wanted something to warm the cockles of my heart.

About three weeks later I got a letter from Tommy Lawrence thanking me personally for going over and above the call of duty. He thanked me profusely and said his surgery had been a success.

There were many other strange incidents during this time of social chaos, but two particularly stick out in my memory. The first came from an exceptionally intelligent sounding Bell Helicopter employee who had been barricaded inside his house by his landlord. He was calling us by phone wondering if we could help him. I asked him why he was being held under house arrest and he said that he had been gone so long that he owed his landlord several months rent in arrears and his landlord was afraid he would take off without paying it and he also wanted him to pay several months in advance now. It was a catch-22 situation because even if he had wanted to comply he needed to go to the bank to get the money. I always found these kind of "Mexican stand-offs" Iranian-style intriguing.

One time when I lived off Karim Khan-e-Zand, I was awoken at about five A.M. by a bunch of obscenity being screamed out in my alley. I stumbled over to open my shutters and stuck my head sleepily out the window, as had several of my neighbors on both sides.

We had six units in our building and we shared a central furnace. Each fall one of the tenants would collect our share of the money from each of us to buy a tank of heating oil. It would take so long to organize this that we would always run out of heating fuel first before we would ever get the stuff delivered, and so we would end up staying warm with little kerosene portable space heaters we called *bokharis*. As I eventually woke up I began to decipher what the argument was all about, complete with some very colorful expletives.

The tenant representative who had taken up the collection had apparently tried to stop the trucker from pumping the fuel oil into our tank because he had only brought half of what we had ordered. The delivery person tried in vain to explain that his truck was only big enough to haul half the fuel at a time and he would have to come back with the second installment subsequent to this first partial shipment. The self-installed tenant representative could be heard saying: "Just what kind of a fool do you take me for? If I let you unload and go, we will never see you again let alone the second installment of our order!"

The truck driver finally reached critical mass on the frustration scale and he lost it: "If I didn't come here to deliver oil what did I come here for, to fuck your mothers? You had better let me unload this heating oil or I am going to come upstairs and line up every female in your building in the halls with their backs to me, every single one of them, your wives, your daughters, and your grandmothers, and I am going to fuck every single one of them, do you understand?"

I started cracking up! I believe he would have, too! I don't know what it was about this apartment, but every month when the rent became due another little skirmish would take place, regular as clockwork. There was a young couple who owned my apartment. Sirous was an opium addict, which I am told causes impotence. Each month as the rent came due he would race to get to my apartment ahead of his wife because he wanted the rent money to buy drugs. He would always lock himself in my bathroom for a long time and I can only imagine he was shooting up in there since I never smelled any heroin smoke.

His wife, on the other hand, would race to try to beat him to my apartment because she wanted a chance to be alone with me. This was a rather scary proposition to me because she had one of those continuous eyebrows that connects in the middle and which Persians think is the evil eye and she had more hair on her arms than I do—and sometimes I have to push mine aside with my hand to see my watch face.

I was caught in the middle of this tug of war for half a year. Finally one month when they had both shown up at the same time at my threshold, in exasperation throwing my hands in the air, I pleaded, "Isn't there some address I could mail a rent check to every month and save you the trouble?"

Well, going back to my tenant under house arrest, I went over to his address and found the barricaded house and talked my way in. I spent a long time talking to the dark-haired, handsome young American. He turned out to be quite an amateur herpetologist and had been off collecting Persian lizards and snakes for all these months he had been away with some well-known naturalist. Once we figured out how many months rent he owed, I set about trying to find the landlord, but according to his sons, who were manning the barricades, he had gone home. I went and bought a *celokebab* "to go" for the poor guy, and when I was bringing it back the neighbors across the street called me over and invited me into their house. It had gold and marble all over the place and stain glass in typical *arriviste* style. The owner turned out to be an Iranian Supreme Court justice, and when I explained the situation he went out and screamed and slapped a few heads around and in no time we had the employee liberated. I guess the revolution wasn't far enough along so he was still able to inspire some fear and awe, but he probably got himself black listed. I thanked him profusely and he said that any time I needed anything I should call him. I heard that a lot in Iran where everyone is a chief and there are no Indians.

Another time I got a call from Ed Miller, a former NYC police detective who was the one Bell Helicopter security officer I really liked. He asked me to go to the address of a certain employee, Steve Jacobs, to see if he was there. He had failed to report in to work for a week and his Vietnamese girl-friend was calling in, concerned about his disappearance. I went by cab to the address. It was a walk up on the second floor. I knocked on the door and heard nothing. I tried the knob and it turned. I opened the door cautiously and peered inside. There was this little man all hunched up in his chair with his back to the door. He was scared to death and finally, after showing him my I.D., I got him calmed down enough to talk. I asked him what the hell was going on. He told me that last week a group of plain clothes police had taken his passport and ordered him not to leave his apartment and not to use the phone.

This sounded pretty fishy to me, so I radioed Ed Miller who then called the central police H.Q. and had them check their records, only to find that no such detail had been assigned to any of their officers nor was any exchange of this kind on record. I told the employee that the men who took his passport were not policemen but friends of the landlord who probably thought that he was planning to leave. In fact he had been planning to move in with his Viet-namese girlfriend. I told him to go back to packing his stuff, go through with his move to his girlfriend's place, and to report to work the next day and that the real police would take care of getting his passport back from his soon-to-be ex-landlord.

Half of my time before and during the revolution was spent sorting out messes employees got themselves into of this nature. Landing in Tehran Air-port without a visa, expired white book immigration visas for Vietnamese rel-atives of dependants of American employees seeking entry to the US for the first time, when the books could only be re-issued in Washington, DC— all these kinds of bureaucratic catch-22 situations of both American and Iranian authorship.

By now, in the course of the events leading up to and into the revolution, we had taken over the Tehran Hilton Hotel as our staging area and had rented rooms there so we did not have to return to home or office in violation of the six P.M. curfew.

One day we heard what sounded like a parade proceeding up Pahlavi Boulevard. We turned on the radio and learned that revolutionaries had captured several military bases and were headed for Niavaran palace. As the parade got closer and the noise level of the singing and the cheers rose, we went out on our balcony, from which we could see that it was a long column made up of tanks and armored cars swarming with civilians waving at the bystanders along the sidewalks. We cheered and waved back although they were probably too far down below our vantage point from the hilltop Hilton for them to hear. We did hear someone above us clear his throat, and we looked up to see retired Generals M and S, second and third in command of Bell Helicopter, and their aide de camps glowering down at us...oooops!

We went back inside the room, and in the middle of the government broadcast of events, the radio went dead. After a few minutes of silence a voice rang out dramatically over the radio. It said: "This is the voice of the Iranian Revolution. We have succeeded in capturing the following army bases...and.... We are asking all those interested in helping to liberate Niavaran Palace to come to...to be issued weapons and join in the glorious revolution."

We turned on the TV in time to see Mammad, my friend, the newscaster, looking nervously over his shoulder at some scuffle going on off screen as he tried to announce the news, and then suddenly he got up, bowed to the audience, and ran off the set, leaving it blank...with only the sound of gun fire in the background.

That night we got a call from the martial law authorities warning us that the revolutionaries would be sending over a few advance men to case the joint later that evening with plans of taking over the Hilton and all the other major international hotels the very next day. They must have had a revolutionary mole on their pay roll to have had this information. It was impressive when you consider that all through the revolution no one ever seemed to know who was doing what to whom and we all used to listen to BBC late night short wave broadcasts to try to determine which forces were responsible for what events of the day before. I went to see *Close Encounters of the Third Kind* one night and the next day that very movie theatre got blown up. Soon thereafter all the movie theatre owners shut down and boarded or bricked over their entrances, but nobody knew who was doing it. Hundreds of parked cars were burned. Armenian liquor stores had all their booze pulled out into the street and smashed, but no one knew who was doing it.

The employees and dependants of Bell Helicopter, Inc., were told to get to the Hilton under their own recognizance and from there we would take responsibility for getting them out of the country. One day I heard what sounded like an auditorium full of people clapping at someone's speech outside the ballroom where we were working. Then I noticed that bullet holes started appearing in lines at the top of the glass curtain wall of the ballroom. What had sounded like applause was small caliber automatic weapons fire, which I had never before heard. We immediately started piling tables turned on their sides and chairs up against the glass side of the room to act as a barricade, and we kept working. That night, in addition to the bullets coming in through the top of the glass, the power failed. Everyone dropped to the carpet, keeping their places in the out processing line, and we handed out candles, the light from which they were able to use to keep filling out their forms prone on the floor.

We had the consul general come to the Hilton, Barabara Belsito, to do her paperwork, which kept us from having to get people or paperwork across town to the US Consulate. That night when I went to the elevator to return to my room I saw some strangers with guns prowling about the hall and then I ran right into Sohrab in the same elevator coming out as I went in. He still looked like Elvis Presley only with an AK-47. He had been dispatcher for our fleet of office drivers. He refused to acknowledge that he knew me.

One time at our office at Jordan Avenue, I had innocently offered half of a pizza we had ordered in for a working lunch but been unable to consume entirely to the drivers whose waiting room was right next to our bullpen. Sohrab, who was their dispatcher, had complained to upper management that I had insulted his men by offering them leftovers and I was requested by management to make a formal apology in front of him and all the drivers. I tried to explain that I had not offered them leftovers but rather to share half our pizza with us, but they were not to be convinced and I ended up biting my lip and making the apology against my better judgement, just to make my boss happy. So to see surly Sohrab wandering the halls of the Hilton with an automatic rifle did not bode well. He used to be an oil worker at Kharg Island, so he said. His English was pretty fluent, complete with a southern accent. I found it ironic as much as he hated us that he imitated Elvis in his mannerisms and speech and hair. I got to my room and shut the door to find a few bullet holes in my window. I used a penknife to dig the splattered flat lead out of the walls of my room up behind my bed on which I stood to reach them. I kept the lead as a souvenir which I later had sealed into a little plastic sphere at the end of a chain to wear around my neck.

I wasn't sure what lay in store for us in the morning and could hardly sleep a wink that night. In fact our department secretary couldn't sleep either and ended up sleeping in my boss's room with him for fear of spending that night by herself. I hoped her boyfriend wouldn't show up too early the next morning looking for her.

Photo by Michel Setboun, Corbis photos, Civilians and Soldiers reconciled.

Photo by Michel Setboun, Corbis Photos, Civilians manning captured tank.

Photo by Michel Setboun, Corbis photos, Civilian triumph.

CHAPTER ELEVEN

Two Days in Tehran in 1979

DAY ONE

As I recall in mid-morning on January 16, 1979, my new driver, Hossein, whom the company had hired for me, with his orange taxi with a fringe of dingo balls around the tops of the windows and a clear blue acrylic sun visor on top of the windshield, and I were trying to get across town. The crowd in the streets was all around us like we had been engulfed by a vast herd of sheep reminiscent of when I was a boy with my family driving back roads in Greece. I had never seen so many people out dancing in the street in my life, and it went on all day. I found myself waving and smiling at the crowd and making the peace sign with both of my hands. Drivers had tied white ribbons on their windshield wipers and had clicked them forward so the wipers did not touch the glass when they swept from left to right, waving the white ribbons like cheering flags. I had never seen so many laughing, happy, jubilant, dancing people anywhere before in my life.

It was the culmination of months of fighting, months of shouting, "Marg Bar Shah!" (Death to the King!) from the rooftops after curfew, from the voices of many millions of souls. How must that man have been feeling at that moment, looking from his airplane at Mount Damavand sticking through the cloud cover for the last time? How had he managed to lose the popular support, which was the only support he had ever really had from the time he handed the former serfs land grants? The old aristocracy had never liked him.

Where had he gone wrong? He had stopped appearing in public and had started sending a life-size photo of himself in his limo instead on the day of the annual parade, celebrating the put-down of the revolt in Azerbaijan in 1947. He had become inaccessible to the people and in desperation, he had

Photo by Thomas Hoepker, Magnum Photos, Cow towing in the 1960's.

Photo by Thomas Hoepker, Magnum Photos, Land grants.

appointed Shahrpour Bakhtiar as Prime Minister, a man who had opposed him his entire career. It was Bakhtiar who asked him to leave; it was Bakhtiar who forbade the troops from firing on public assemblies. I often wonder if the Shah had not ordered his troops to fire on the people if things might have gone differently. Certainly rubber bullets, tear gas, and even salt would not have created the martyrs the blood-loving, self-serving Khomeini craved—a man who wasn't even of Iranian origin. But then what poison had the Shah sewn within his subjects with his SAVAK and their tortures, rapes, and executions? They say SAVAK raped Ayatollah Taleghani's daughter and forced him to watch. "As you sew, so shall you reap...." He had allowed no loyal opposition. And the ways of dictatorship and tyranny and revenge his subjects had learned well. During and after the revolution, people would break into the houses of known former Savakis and pull them out of their chairs at their dinner table and out into the street. They would proceed to stone them to death right in front of their families.

Poor Bakhtiar, a well-educated man who could have led a secular Iran into a great era of democracy, basically signed his own death sentence by accepting the position. Did he do it because he thought it was his patriotic duty?

Photo by Abbas, Magnum Photos, list of Savak victims on US Embassy wall while hostages are inside.

Photo by Abbas, Magnum Photos, pro Shah demonstration.

Photo by Abbas, Magnum Photos, Pro Shah demonstration at Amjediyeh Stadium

Photo by Abbas, Magnum Photos, Anti Shah demonstration

Photo by Alain Nogues, Corbis Sygma Photo, Shahrpour Balehtiar

Day Two
Enter the Dragon

February 1, 1979. When I got up and went outside, Tehran was a ghost town. Not a creature was stirring—in fact, there was no movement, no sound. I remember the only motion that caught my eye was a dead leaf twirling around in a little dust devil from a breeze in the middle of the street. It was as if the city of millions had become a ghost town or perhaps all humanity had been wiped out by radiation. It could have been a warning of the endless rounds of death, torture, and execution, which were to come....

It was ironic that on the day the Shah left, everyone was dancing in the street, which it seems they should have been doing on this day if this new leader had come with love in his heart, forgiveness, and peace, but instead, Tehran was like a cemetery that day: empty of human life. I didn't even see cats or dogs. The reason the city was deserted, of course, was because the masses had gone out to the airport to witness his arrival.

I never saw Khomeini smile. His dark angry eyebrows were like thunder clouds, sinister and frightening to me in all of the posters and photos of him, which had been plastered all about even in bank windows in hopes of not being broken by bricks. If he represented God at all, it was only His wrath.

What if, similar to Nelson Mandela, who after thirty years in prison, ushered in the end of Apartheid in South Africa by calling for a general amnesty? What if Khomeini had done that? What if the new leader of Iran had won a Nobel Peace Prize?

And why is this man smiling?

Photo by Abbas, Magnum Photos, Bazargan and Entezam. Why is this man smiling?

Photo by Abbas, Magnum Photos, Khomeini arrives

CHAPTER TWELVE

In Freefall

ALL MORNING DIFFERENT REVOLUTIONARY GROUPS HAD BEEN FIGHTING over the National Iranian Radio and Television station the next hill over from where we were at the Hilton. Each group knew that whoever captured and controlled the station could go on the airwaves and claim authorship of the revolution.

The Bell Helicopter employees were taking a break from the lines and from filling out paperwork for the out-processing by going to the lunch room where the Hilton had set up a nice buffet. I asked my boss, Neil, what we were going to tell the employees about the imminent attack. He said, "Nothing! We will welcome the revolutionaries with open arms and make them feel at home. That is our best strategy!" I was amazed once again by Neil. He was so smart beyond his years. I remember studying in anthropology about how the sedentary Pueblo and Hopi Indians would set up huge feasts before the attacks of the warlike nomadic Comanche Indians so that instead of offering resistance they would welcome them home like heroes and give them such a party they would forget about making war.

Neil couldn't have been twenty-four years old when I knew him and he was the head of an entire department of employee relations, which included a travel agency. I remember I was three years older than him. He had very cold dry hands, pale skin, and dark hair, and he spoke Farsi very well indeed. I will never forget the first time I shook his hand at the end of my job interview. It was a reluctant handshake devoid of feeling, almost like shaking hands with something inanimate, like a sheath of Xerox paper. He was quite reserved, aloof and unemotional, almost British, when you first met him, but once you got to know him he had a wicked sense of humor combined with a love for theatre, and we would often make up completely impromptu fantasies on the spot, just riding on a bus for example. We would pretend to be

Neil Fucci, Esfahan 1976
photo by Byron Edelen

bank robbers whispering out loud, plotting our next heist just to see how the passengers around us would try to studiously ignore us while they died of curiosity inside, we liked to imagine. Once I got to be friends with Neil, I understood a lot of his superficial reserve was his defensive coloration for being gay. The security gorillas had once tried to plant dope in his desk and get him shipped home after one of the young Persian drivers had complained about him making unwanted advances. All that scandal was well before I came on board and I always try to let bygones be bygones as they say, but security had a permanent hard-on for him, being homophobes from East Texas. Neil subtly taught me, often by unspoken example, many things about human nature, about public relations, about corporate politics, about bravado, about overcoming fear and taking risks for the right reasons, about keeping a positive attitude and optimism, and all about life's infinite possibilities. Eventually we became such good friends that I would sometimes pass a pleasant evening smoking opium or hash with him out on his patio lying next to one another on a mattress thrown outside on the floor, peacefully watching the clouds play over the moon and talking about what we wanted to do with our lives after Iran. The fact that I was straight and he was gay never interfered with our friendship, although I got the impression on occasion that he did appear with me in public to make his boyfriends jealous. Once when we were stoned we went to eat at Maxim's de Tehran, and when he cut into his chicken Kievski, hot melted cheese squirted out making him gasp, only slightly, barely audibly. Weeks later he confessed to me that in that instant he had wet himself. He was never afraid of life like some of us are. He seemed so in his element and comfortable with life, as if no situation could ever produce panic in him, perhaps a headache was as bad as it would get. He was at home with the seediest side of society as well as the most refined, and he was a gourmet chef to boot. In his kitchen he taught me to make an orange soufflé complete with the brown paper chimney cut out from a grocery bag so it wouldn't tilt over as it rose in the oven and on another occasion salmon mousse. If friends wanted to throw a Greek theme party, we would set to work and in no time churn out a hundred dolma. All in all he was a wonderful human being who in retrospect it was my great privilege to know...and I am left wondering how someone so young had come to be so wise.

At any rate, on this particular occasion on the eve of our being taken hostage he imparted an incredible calm. I don't know where some people find their courage, but I have come to learn in the school of life, each of us has a different capacity for bravery and some of the most courageous people of all do not fit the stereotype, the archetypal God of War, Ares *not*.... Sometimes they are the complete antithesis, like Gandhi.

About an hour after lunch, we started to hear what was to become that characteristic sound of many people clapping outside the hotel; it sounded like they were applauding a speaker, but it was not applause; it

141

was automatic weapons fire. The bullet holes started silently appearing in neat rows across the top of the glass curtain wall of the ballroom where we were working. I ran out of the room, across the lobby, and headed for the front door but it was under siege. There was a shoot out going on between two groups over that front door. I pushed my way between some revolutionaries busy returning rifle fire in the doorway to have a look for myself. The little puffs of smoke led my eyes to where I could see a sniper crouched in some bushes on the side of a hill across from the hotel entrance shooting at us. I ran downstairs to the kitchen to search for another way out. It occurred to me that there might be a food delivery chute but there wasn't. I went to the laundry room to see if there was a laundry delivery chute. None! Then I found a hall that led to a fire tunnel exit but it was padlocked. Shit! I was determined not to get caught, but unbelievably there was no way out except by the front door! I tried to open the windows on the ground floor on the side opposite the front door, but they weren't even designed to open. The Hilton was on a hilltop and so there was a considerable drop, too far to jump down to the ground, from the first story windows on the south side, which is probably why they weren't meant to open. In retrospect I could have taken a fire axe from it case in the hall and broken open one of the windows, but when shit starts happening you try to cling to what you know and smashing windows just wasn't something that I had ever had to do in an emergency so it didn't even occur to me now.

Finally all that I could think to do was go into an adjacent ballroom that wasn't being used and keep the lights turned off and sit on the carpet in a corner under a table in the hope that if I remained quiet enough I would escape notice until I could somehow find an opportunity to escape later after the siege was over. At least this would buy me some time to think. As I sat quietly in the dark listening to my own breathing, I began to become aware of some other breathing and then the snuffling of weeping. It was a woman's weeping. I said quietly, "Who is there?"

"It is Mahaste," came the reply. She was one of our Iranian staffers from our head quarters building. "My husband told me not to come to work today. It said on the radio that the revolutionaries would be capturing the main hotels. He was right, I shouldn't have come. O boo-hoo-hoo...."

I said, "Please, Mahaste Khanoum, don't make noise or they will find us. Please stop crying...."

The very next minute two armed toughs opened the door and flipped on the lights and then herded us at gunpoint into the main ballroom where everyone else was sitting on the floor with their knees up and with their hands folded behind their heads and elbows up in the air, in that classic prisoner formation as if we were waiting to do sit ups in a gym class. Everyone was quiet and numb in the shock of disbelief. Our captors frisked us for arms and took my walkie-talkie and eventually all the walkie-talkies.

Next they rounded us up into a line and started marching us down the stairs into the fire tunnel. It was at this point that one of our captors said in good American English: "We have nothing against the American people but we do not like the policies of your government." I remember thinking that most of us had no idea what the policies of our government were, especially the classified ones of the CIA that these revolutionaries found so offensive. They went on to apologize for having to use us to make a political statement. I noted that they were all very young, in their teens.

About halfway through the tunnel there was a sudden commotion, a ripple in the crowded line, and then we stopped moving, like a traffic jam in rush hour. Another group of revolutionaries had forced open the fire tunnel door from the outside and were proceeding toward us. Thinking we were trying to escape, since they couldn't see our captors who were behind us, they started pointing their guns and prodding with bayonets at us to stop us from moving forward while the revolutionaries in the back were prodding to keep us from going backward. It was like some kind of a scene from Dante's Inferno, like poor damned souls being prodded by devils with little pitchforks in the dark throat of hell mouth. We told our captors to please make up their minds which way they wanted us to go, and finally they decided to take us back to the main ballroom and return us to the fetal sitting position with hands behind heads again.

It was about this time that, being good Iranians even if they were our captors, they decided it was time to be good hosts and feed us even though we had all just eaten lunch. They raided the hotel kitchen and brought us up all kinds of food: chicken and rice and cucumbers and barbari bread, accompanied by the usual. "*Bokhor, bokhor*, eat, eat!" I tried to explain that we had already eaten lunch but it was useless. I mean, like, who has an appetite anyway, even if we hadn't just eaten, when one is taken hostage anyway, right?

I heard the Bell Helicopter security officers muttering to each other that if only they could wrestle a few guns away from the revolutionaries, they could take back the hotel for us Rambo style. I remember thinking: "O God, if anyone is going to get us killed, it is going to be these baboons!" Just then I looked up in time to see Neil with a white revolutionary headband like them, walking full stride up the middle of the room to the front where he proceeded to bark out orders to our captors. I thought to myself: "What the hell is he up to?" Then it struck me, it was brilliant, brilliant like Neil, and I wish I could have had this segment on film. He told me later that he had noticed a dearth of leadership among the young revolutionaries, so doing what he did best, which was people management, he had decided to take over.

I watched in utter amazement as they began following his orders. It was like a Jedi mind trick. Neil had figured out that as long as we were all herded together in one big room, all 800 of us, it would be too easy for our captors to just eliminate us with sprays of automatic weapons fire or else herd us *en*

143

masse to a prison or former military base and hold us there for ransom. Neil talked the revolutionaries into letting us go back to our rooms individually, which would make it harder for them to shoot us all or move us all together as a group to a prison. He had us form a single file while the revolutionaries frisked each one of us again before sending us off to our rooms. I noticed that there were also two or three gun moll types—really attractive but hard-looking revolutionary babes with bandoliers of bullets and Uzis, accompanying the young toughs, and it was rumored that they made love to the Mojaheddin guerilla fighters indiscriminately, as part of their support for the revolution, but I don't know if this were true. Considering how heavily armed they were, I think they were making their own choices of mates, not the other way round.

Only a few of us had cleared the inspection when suddenly there was a flurry and in strode my assistant Jamshid with two revolutionaries prodding him in the back with their rifles. He said he had come to help us. I was scared for him because he had been a former Savak and was married to a Christian Armenian girl and he shouldn't have come here. At one point he spun round on his heels and started screaming at the two revolutionary guards who were bird-dogging him: "You, quit sticking me in the back with those bayonets, understand?! Why don't you just shoot me and get it over with!" About this time Neil and I jumped Jamshid simultaneously and literally shoved a sock in his mouth! We whispered in his ears that we had things under control and he needed to get calmed down. Eventually we un-gagged him and he took to sulking. The revolutionaries went back to frisking us one by one and sending us back to our rooms with Neil issuing directives all the while.

Then, perhaps only ten minutes after this, there was another little flurry of activity and suddenly, totally unexpectedly on my part, in sashayed my friend Pouran with two gunmen carrying Uzis at each side. She caught my eyes with hers and made straight for me through the crowd. There were armed revolutionaries backing up in front of her with their guns aimed at her and her entourage as she trudged forward unphased by them. When she came up to me in the line, she stopped and with a swagger planted her feet splayed apart in front of me and, crossing her arms, barked out at the revolutionaries: "This is Rasool, he is a Moslem, he is a friend of my family, and he has nothing to do with these Americans. We are taking him away from here right now. And if you try to stop us, we will shoot it out right now!"

I felt myself instantly grow quite pale and rasped out: "Pouran, we had things under control here, what are you trying to do, get me killed?"

She turned on me almost venomously and hissed: "You shut up! I know what I am doing. Do you really think they will die shooting it out over the likes of you, dear? Don't flatter yourself!"

I felt stung but she was right. Our adversaries took one look at me, then at her automatic sub machine guns, and then at their own semi-automatic rifles, and without a word they all fell back a few steps and made room for us to pass. Pouran, giving me a satisfied look, then stopped and barked at them once more: "And furthermore, not only are we taking him out of here but we are going to stop by his room and collect his things on the way out!" What she knew and I didn't yet was that as we were being held hostage down in the main ballroom, the revolutionaries were sacking our rooms. I found out later that one of them had come across one of our female employee's bras in the drawers of her room and, spreading them out over her bed, had ejaculated over them.

Anyway, after collecting my things we took the elevator back downstairs and strode through the lobby, the four of us unopposed. A group of American employees, who knew me casually, who were still being held called out to me as we passed by: "Where are they taking you? Are they letting us go now?" I had this sudden mental image of someone yelling fire in a movie theatre and starting a stampede or a drowning person grabbing hold of a swimmer and pulling him under, too, so with words that sprang from my chest unpremeditated and yet strangely familiar, as if rehearsed, I shouted back, "No, I am being taken out for interrogation!" That immediately stopped any thoughts of charging toward the front door which they might have had as we quickly passed out into the sunshine.

My hours of being hostage were suddenly over as if they had never happened. Kids were playing kick ball in the street outside. Women were shopping for flowers with laden baskets in their arms. Old men were drinking tea and reading the paper as if nothing at all were any different, while inside the hotel about 800-1 (less me) people were still being held hostage. One of our gunmen brought a big SUV Jeep around and we all piled in and drove over to the next hill to the Dumas apartment tower where she lived. When we got inside her apartment, it was all I could do to thank her, when she launched into our next mission of the day, which was apparently to go with her hired guns over to the Gasr political prison and help liberate it. I had heard that the prisoners were locked underground and the approach to the electronic door had been mined by the retreating guards. The door was like one of those bank vaults programmed to only open on a certain day at a certain time.

I told Pouran I doubted if the revolutionaries would take too kindly to an American showing up at the prison, and besides I had quite enough excitement for one day. Pouran got angry with me then. She had had a lot of therapy and in the past she had often launched into long rambling soliloquies about how her parents were slowly poisoning her and her sister was poisoning her. The supposed motives were very complicated and convoluted and I could never sort them out, but it had something to do with their allegedly trying to gain custody of her little girl. Now that I wouldn't go with her to help liberate Gasr Prison, she quickly turned on me and began accusing me of poisoning her as well. I began to realize that where she had found the courage to do what she had just done for me was in her madness and I felt bad for her.

145

She left her apartment with me in it. Ranting and raving, she motioned her gunmen out the door and slammed it behind her, and although I didn't know it at the time that would be the last that I would ever see of her.

I sat there for a few minutes merely trying to digest everything that had just transpired. Here I was in the peace and quiet of her luxury apartment with a view above the clouds from the top of our hill looking down Jordan Avenue towards downtown. The sky was light blue and sunlight sparkled in the reflector pools from the hidden walled gardens of Tehran. I could see pigeons and starlings winging about down below me. Quietly a little voice inside me started wondering about my friends like Neil, Charlie, and Jim who were still being held hostage in the Hilton. Finally I couldn't ignore that voice any longer and I called the Hilton.

As if nothing at all were going on, the hotel operator transferred me to the front desk and the front desk had Neil paged for me. Amazingly, Neil was actually able to come to the phone. I had rehearsed a little speech in the mirror before I called and now I tried it out: "Hi, Neil, I guess you must be disappointed in me for abandoning you guys but I figured being taken hostage wasn't in my job description. Anyway I'm sorry...."

"Yeah, you're right it was a shitty thing to do!" he replied and the started snickering.

"What are you laughing about at a time like this, Neil?" says I.

"Well, do you remember how the three security pigs were trying to go Rambo on us and take back the hotel?"

"Yeah! What did you do to them, Neil? Tell me!"

"Well, I told the revolutionaries that they were CIA agents and they have them locked up in the basement sitting back to back in a circle on the floor tied elbow to elbow." And with that Neil started laughing mischievously again. "They are going to be taking General M and his wife and our three 'CIA agents' down to Khomeini 's headquarters for interrogation and I'm going along to act as interpreter."

The next day it was in the local paper that the revolutionaries had captured three CIA agents. Neil told me that during their interview with Khomeini they had been separated from seeing him directly by a black lace curtain reminiscent of a Roman Catholic confessional. "So what did you guys talk about?" I wanted to know.

"Well, I asked him what they intended to do with all of us now that we had been captured and his reply was: 'Oh, nothing. You are welcome to be our guests in Iran, and if you insist on leaving we will offer you armed escorts to and from Mehrabad Airport if you like!'"

And that is exactly what they did. Every day when we got all our employees and their dependants loaded into our buses and mini-vans, the revolutionaries on motorcycles and packed into Paykans and Iran Chevrolets would ride with our convoy waving their weapons around for the benefit of the spectators.

They also set up a collection point in the lobby of the Tehran Hilton for the return of our looted stuff where we could go and identify it and collect it. Suddenly they became very anxious to keep a good reputation.

But I digress. I spent the night alone in Pouri's apartment. She never did come back that night, and by the next morning I was feeling guilty and starting to miss my friends at Bell Helicopter. So believe it or not I decided to go back to the Hilton where they were being held. No sooner had I stepped back inside the front door of the Hilton lobby than a gunfight started between our revolutionary guards and some snipers on the hill across the way again. In that instant, I couldn't believe how stupid I was for coming back for more of this.

Without a moment's hesitation and knowing from bitter experience that the front door was the only way in our out, I spun on my heels and ran back out the door as bullets ricocheted all around me, and I ran all the way down the hill just as fast as my little legs could carry me weaving from side to side to make me into a more difficult moving target.

Once I got down to Pahlavi Blvd, I hailed a cab and went home. By the next morning I was feeling like a buffalo in stories I had heard about the American Wild West. Even when a buffalo had succeeded in escaping from its stampeding herd to stand and catch its breath, it would inevitably re-enter the fray because without its herd it was at a loss for what to do. So I went back a second time. I made it inside and as far as the main ballroom this time and studiously went back to work helping to out-process employees. Looking at the passenger list of the next group scheduled to go, I saw my name at the very top of the list. I went to Neil and asked him what the hell that was all about. I had no interest in leaving.

Neil replied, "Well, I can't get any work out of you. Every time the shooting starts, you run away. So I might as well send you back to the US." "Well, I'm here now aren't I?" I got his point despite my protest, and ironically I ended up being the last employee to leave Iran, having stayed even after Neil left, the circumstances of which is another story in itself.

About this time a platoon of regular infantry from the US Army hospital showed up looking for our help to be evacuated. I can still see them in their olive drab combat fatigues and camouflage suits armed to the nines with all kind of ordnance and walkie-talkies hanging off their web belts, and we told them that before we could do anything to help them, that the revolutionary guards would be collecting all their weapons. This must have been very humiliating for them but it was not negotiable. That night what a picture it was to see an entire platoon of US Army sleeping in their sleeping bags on the floor of the lobby of the Tehran Hilton because we had run out of rooms, where only a few months before, Touss and I had been lounge lizards and the prior spring Uncle Mamdahli had taken us for an "all you can eat" and drink, caviar, champagne, and fillet mignon New Year's dinner at the elegant Chez Michelle restaurant in there. The American soldiers were very appreciative of our help actually. I believe that it was during their brief stay on the lobby floor that Conrad Hilton died of a heart attack in the news and I remember wondering if the Tehran Hilton being changed into a detention center had anything to do with it.

During the months of December 1978 and January 1979 we managed to evacuate over three thousand employees and dependants out of Iran from our staging area at the Hilton. We also managed to smuggle out a few British subjects, including one colorful blowhard quack named Michael Pelham who claimed to be a movie producer, and also a few Iranian nationals who had life threatening reasons to want to leave. Neil and I felt good about that, like we had earned some Brownie points somewhere on the big score board up in the sky.

Meanwhile on the national scene beyond our microcosm, the Shah's pick, poor Sharpour Bakhtiar's government, had come and gone and Mehdi Bazargan, who was Khomeini's pick, was trying it on for size. Some dirt bag from the University of Miami bearing the same last name and claiming to be his relative showed up at our offices at Jordan Avenue looking for a job. The revolutionaries had let a group of about five of us from Bell Helicopter move all the company and employee files to a single building there which had been our headquarters and from which we worked.

I knew that the owner of this building was in prison, having been one of the Shah's generals, and so whenever nobody else was around I was on the phone calling long distance to school friends in Italy, the USA, and Tokyo, talking for hours, yucking it up. I knew that the billing system had been totally messed up during the revolution and I would probably be long gone by the time it was sorted out, especially with the owner in jail.

At any rate, "Miami" Bazargan Jr. was given the assignment of trying to collect some of the company assets in various bank accounts around Iran. He headed down to Isfahan and that was the last we ever saw of him. Several months later his sister and his mom were in my office crying their eyes out and claiming that it was all our fault and that we must do something to help. I managed to get them calmed down enough to explain to me what was happening. Apparently the revolutionary committee down in Isfahan had allowed "Miami" to withdraw all the Bell Helicopter money from our corporate accounts there, but then the temptation proved too great for the revolutionaries. The minute he was in possession of several million dollars in his attaché case they nabbed him, accused him of grand theft, slapped him in jail, and confiscated the money in the name of the Iranian people, and in jail he had been now for months with no prayer of reprieve. The American knucklehead they had left in charge of the skeleton crew, which was now five of us, had no clue what to do to help. I went back to talking to mom and sister, and together we decided I should write a letter on Bell Helicopter letterhead, get it notarized, and explain in it that he had been authorized to act on our behalf

148

as our power of attorney in fact in disposing of these funds. I'm not sure what happened because I left country without hearing anything more; however, at least mom and sister left dry-eyed with my letter and a thin ray of hope.

Very strange situations arise in the aftermath of revolutions, in the aftermath of mass civil disobedience and the break down of law and order and infrastructure such as police. The jails emptied out during this time of both criminals and political prisoners. Caviar and opium and automatic weapons were traded and flowed like water since all regulations broke down. People laundered money, sold traveler's checks, forged passports, and smuggled in goods normally subject to tariffs in their cars every day from Iraq and Turkey for a living. Ever resourceful, all kinds of new enterprises sprang up, like the auctioning off of the contents of rich people's houses who had either left country, been executed, or were rotting in jail. Sometimes the revolutionary auctioneers would forget to invite anyone and back up a truck at official closing time to freeload the stuff for themselves.

Our Iranian lady office manager at our headquarter's building had worked for us for twenty years and received a $35,000 severance check which the revolutionaries got wind of and jailed her, at which point we complained to another revolutionary committee who in turn got her released and jailed the group that had jailed her. "These were the best of times and the worst of times!"

Then there were the "Laissez Passer" bunch I would have to help out. These were usually Vietnamese or Thai women and children, in-laws of some Bell Helicopter employee, who did not have US citizenship or even residency yet and whose white immigration booklets had expired during the chaos before they could get out in time to use them to enter the USA. The catch-22 was that these booklets, once they had expired, could only be re-issued from Washington DC. So, oh, dear me, what to do, what to do? I don't know how I figured it out, maybe one of my US Embassy or Counselor friends told me, but I would send them to the German Embassy to get a one-time travel document called a "Laissez Passer" which allowed the bearer to go from country A and to country B once with this document. Once they were able to get to Germany, they could register with the US Embassy and wait for Washington DC, to send them a new one via the Embassy's diplomatic pouch. At least they were out of the "war zone." Of course it was always dicey trying to get the custom's officers at the Mehrabad Airport to accept this form of document as a valid passport and allow my charges to board. I would always hold my breath when they would stand in line to get these papers stamped with exit visas. I got way too much experience explaining what they were to these officials, who only felt comfortable with little booklet shaped passports not flat sheet of paper equivalents.

I spent days shredding documents and photos for a group of Bell Helicopter die hards hanging out in Athens waiting for an opportunity to sell the revolutionaries on a new contract to at least properly store and maintain the two thousand aircraft helicopter fleet if they weren't going to fly them. Apparently aircraft have to be stored properly with special oils and so forth and can't be left parked out on airstrips immobile for long periods of time. We even set about trying to re-establish contact with all our Iranian counterparts who had been trained as helicopter mechanics and pilots so we could rehire them if our delegation were successful. By this point in time Khomeini was embarrassed by all the foreigners leaving even though he had invited them to stay and so he decided that in order to save face that they should all leave. They were not interested in Bell Helicopter's offer; they were not interested in showing any need for foreign assistance in their own affairs. In fact the newspapers panned the Bell offer and criticized the Shah for "spending the Iranian people's money on aging American military hardware." This of course was not true since these aircraft were state of the art and some had been specially designed and developed for high altitude and rapidly changing altitude for Iran, which is quite mountainous in certain regions.

The arduous task of documenting all the employees' claims coming in from back in the USA for lost wages, vacation days, and personal assets and household effects had finally come to an end. So, too, the documentation of corporate bank accounts that the revolutionaries had frozen. I was to later learn that any contracts between the government of the United States and a government of any other nation which were to be subcontracted to private American companies were insured by the US government with a certain percent of money held in escrow which, in the event of revolution or expulsion, could be used to pay claims of losses from these subcontractors on a first-come first-serve basis, which is why they were in such a hurry to get the documentation done. I remember trudging to work at the H.Q. on Jordan Avenue in the snow and then spending the day working through the file cabinets with long lists of telex messages, trying to match up names and employee numbers with their files and then trying to glean enough info from within them to either corroborate or deny their claims.

We had some comical exchanges with the revolutionary guards who had been assigned to our building. I remember arriving one day in time to see our young guard at the desk in the lobby hide away a *Playboy* magazine and then proceed to proudly inform me that he had arrested a young couple he had caught making out in their car in our parking lot the night before. I told him they were only doing what he wished he could do! He didn't like that much. Then another day, two guards came to me and asked me what all the boxes were in a certain storeroom. I went with them to look and, to my surprise, it was wall to wall Christmas boxes of fruitcakes from Texas, which, what with the revolution coming, the employees had not bothered to collect this year. The boxes reached almost to the ceiling and when you opened the door you were confronted with a solid wall of them. I explained that they were a special kind of cake that Americans ate on our Christmas holidays. I went back to work and about an hour later I passed by the room and found the two revolutionary guards had opened one and were eating great pieces of it, unaware that it was rum soaked. I had a good chuckle over that one.

One day Neil finally decided to leave. I went with him down to a former Savak office where the former Savaki agents told us that in order to get an exit visa he needed documentation that he had committed no crimes against the Iranian people and owed no taxes and this should come in the form of a letter from our former Iranian sponsor. Well, we had a problem with that because our former Iranian sponsor was the late General Khosrodad, chief of the army avionics, whom the revolutionaries had executed.

It was in the tabloids just to prove to the masses that he was really dead. He had a handsome physique of which he had been very proud and for which he had worked out in the gym on a regular basis, making him look like a man in his thirties rather than his fifties despite the white hair. He had been cocky and full of life and arrogance, strutting like a peacock, bragging in public addresses about his philandering. Now his body lay there on the ground in the photo pumped full of bullet holes like a Swiss cheese. He and a friend had been captured while trying to escape piloting their own small plane. I'm not sure what his list of crimes had been. I had heard he had helped put down an insurrection in Azerbaijan once, killing thousands of people. Who knows...anyone from the Shah's regime was a target because the people were so afraid that if they left any of them alive, they would plot to overthrow the revolutionaries and bring back the King.

It was understandable that violence begat violence, especially when it had been repressed for fifty years and had been simmering like a volcano all that time. Still it was horrific to see photos in the tabloids of people I had known, like Dr. Said Said, speaker of the lower house of parliament, a gracious man whom I had once had a picnic with, with his friends and family, near Dezin, with a menu composed only of romaine lettuce heads, one for each of us, with our own little bowls for dipping in honey vinegar dressing. Now he, too, was in the tabloids lying dead on the ground pumped so full of lead it looked like a bad case of measles. I would fight to hold back my tears as I would overhear the list of executions each day on the drive in to work on the car radio while my fundamentalist driver relished it all. Strange world it had become, rather like the Reign of Terror in post-revolutionary France, I should imagine.

One day Khomeini's son woke up Abbas Hoveidi, the Shah's former prime minister, in his prison cell, held a pistol to his head, read his sentence: "You have committed crimes against heaven and earth," and pulled the trigger. This was for being gay. I can remember the age of innocence, the Camelot time, when I was sixteen in 1966 and attended, with Touss, an outdoor banquet in the prime minister's garden, given to welcome back the Iranian students for the summer from their studies abroad on scholarships from the Shah. Mr. Hoveida had personally come down to shake our hands and welcome us.

I never forgot that party because the two tables laden with fruits and pastries and beverages were so long that the ends of them were lost in the crowd of students and it was easier to get to a friend on the other side by crawling under them when no one was looking than by walking around. Hoveida had once written a personal get well card to Touss when he was in the hospital for bone cancer surgery. This was the man they summarily executed without due process of law.

Anyway, regarding the need for a clearance from our late Iranian sponsor, ever resourceful Neil thought about it for all of ten minutes and then told the former Savakis: "I'll be back with your documentation tomorrow." He turned to me and said, "Come on!" We hopped in his car and I said nothing as he drove us up to the far northern end of Tehran to the army avionics base near Niavaran, which I believe was called Lalezon. Somehow he managed to talk our way in, again like using Jedi mind tricks. Then he proceeded to find his way to the office of a colonel, who had once been the General's aide de camp. I don't know how Neil used to do this stuff. He was uncanny. He had never been to this base before and yet it seemed like he could find his way around it sleep walking. Neil had an intuitive ability to deal with bureaucracy no matter of what stripe.

We got to the colonel's office and Neil explained what he needed, and in no time at all, the colonel's staff produced the letter he used to leave Iran. He turned to me and said prophetically: "Pay attention to what we just did, because you may have to do the same thing yourself by the time you leave." We had stayed on for Bell Helicopter at our own risk by now and they had us sign waivers that we understood they were no longer able to guarantee our safety. I ended up actually being the last American Bell employee to leave and probably one of the last Americans to leave Iran.

When I walked down Takht-e-Jamshid Avenue, crowds of children would encircle me staring as if I were an alien from outer space, which I probably was. Once I started speaking Persian to them, they would tell me all kinds of anti-cleric jokes and swear that one day they would hang all the mullahs from the street lights and drag them behind the bumpers of cars. That was twenty-seven years ago now and I am still waiting.

One joke they told me went like this: One day Khomeini and Prime Minister Bazargan were flying in a helicopter down to Qom. Khomeini turned to Bazargan and said, "Mehdi, dear, are you feeling cold?"

"No your holiness, I am just fine, thank you for your concern."

"Don't be shy to tell me if you are actually feeling cold!"

"No, your holiness, I am not just being polite, I assure you I am quite comfortable. But again I thank you for your kindness your saintliness."

"Okay, Mehdi, if you insist you are not cold I accept, but if you change your mind, we can always turn off the fan, so don't be shy," he said pointing up at the propeller.

Finally the day came when I had no more work to do for Bell and foreigners were being asked to leave. I had seen many amazing things in those four months after the revolution, like the 20,000 modern Iranian women who had been the first to march in protest against the mullahist regime. Hooligans on motor scooters had come alongside and jabbed at them with penknives until Khomeini himself had to come on national television to tell the hooligans to stop. The next week he had 2 million peasant women from the countryside bussed in from their villages in their veils, which they had always worn, to march in counter, counter protest. The bussing was the same technique he had learned from his predecessor, the Shah.

There was the day the famous newspaper published a blank edition except for one sentence on the front page which said that due to the current atmosphere of censorship which had returned that they saw no further point in publishing anything. That edition sold out and the next week their newspaper office was burned to the ground.

Meanwhile the crowd was putting the last touches on dismantling the torture house up the street from where I lived on Kuche Khaghani and the Semiramis Hotel on Roosevelt Avenue about two blocks from the US Embassy.

I had watched the butchers go on strike when Khomeini announced that only meat slaughtered in the Islamic way by slitting the throat of the sheep and bleeding it was acceptable. I saw this being done in the gutters of the city streets right downtown. Anyway, the Iranian butchers had to get the Pakistani butcher back in Australia to do a video which they got onto the TV somehow to show Khomeini that the Australian sheep were in fact slaughtered in the Islamic way even if they did arrive frozen to Iran. I remember that week I couldn't find any meat to buy and so finally I decided to buy a sheep's tongue, which was all I could find. I boiled it for a few hours and it was still too tough to cut. Three hours later it was still too tough. Finally I left it to boil all night. When my old Kurdish landlady came up to say goodbye to me she laughed when I told her about the tongue. She explained to me how I was supposed to make a slit and peal off the outer membrane, which was the only tough part. She was right; the inside had turned to mush.

She gave me at least a dozen loolch of opium to take with me on my trip home. All that last week, I would go evenings to Touss's house to receive friends and his relatives who wanted to say goodbye to me in person after five years. My girlfriend Roya was going to be the hardest one to say goodbye to, but it was not easy at all with anyone and we shed many tears.

Sure enough Neil had been right and I eventually found my way back to the colonel's office at the army avionics base. This time he started to obfuscate. I figured I was just not as savvy as Neil. I reminded him that I had been there a month before with Neil and now I needed the same kind of letter. "But I don't know you. How do I know you don't owe taxes and didn't commit any crimes against the Iranian people?"

"Well let me put it to you this way, Colonel, sir, I am going to sit down in the middle of your office on the carpet and I am not leaving until you get me such a letter," and so saying I sat down cross-legged in the middle of his floor space. He was terribly embarrassed and immediately his sergeant started bringing me in pastries and tea. I thanked him and said, "You may bring me all the tea and pastry in Iran, but I am not leaving without that letter."

After about twenty-five minutes working at his desk and pretending to ignore my presence, he peered down at me over his glasses when no one else was present and whispered to me that the problem was that his secretary, in keeping with the spirit of the revolution, was on strike and he couldn't type. I asked him if he would mind if I spoke to her myself and he said all right and pointed her out to me in the next room where a passel of women gadded about the water cooler. I went over to her and politely introduced myself and then explained what I needed and offered to pay her handsomely for the letter, which I did, about twenty dollars, and that was how I got out of Iran. I took it back to the former Savak office; they ran me in their computer once more and then, without any further delay, having remembered me from before with Neil, they stamped an exit visa in my passport.

I spent my last night at Touss's house. One of our good friends whom we had nicknamed Court for his courtly manners had stopped by to say goodbye: "Well, I don't suppose I shall ever be seeing you again...so have a nice life."

That last week I had also run into Khosrow Eghbal, younger brother of the late and great Doctor Manoucher Eghbal, former prime minister and one time president of National Iranian Oil Company, standing in a doorway chatting with an Englishmen to escape the rain as I walked up Shemran Road. I said hello and he responded nonchalantly while all the while I was shocked he would be still in country.

The last person to come to Touss's house was the neighborhood mullah who had come to bless me for a safe voyage. He whispered in my ear: "I hope you don't think all of us Moslems are like these fanatics!" I told him I knew better and returned his hug.

I cried in the taxi all the way to the airport. Roya met me at the gate to say goodbye. She was being quite brave until I called her one of our mutual terms of endearment in Persian and then we both broke down and cried. I gave her one last hug and hoped that she would be able to get out of Iran soon. I told her that once I figured out where I was going to be that I would write to her but right now I had no clue and no job waiting and was headed to spend some time in Samos, Greece, for the summer to write about all this and to decompress.

In the men's room of the airport I found myself flushing all the looleh of opium down the toilet, afraid of what they would do to me either here or at the other end of the flight if I got caught with it. This made me cry too....

On the airplane, which was Iran Air since that was the only airline flying in and out of Iran at that time, who should I run into but our friend George, a British red-headed airline stewardess whom Touss had nicknamed, who use to invite us to the parties she and her stewardess roommates would give. She smiled at me and made sure I got plenty of vodka and orange juice on the flight to Athens.

The next day I was sitting reading the newspaper in Ammonia Square in downtown Athens and the headlines were about the beginning of the Iran-Iraq war. I thought, *Oh, God, how much more must my adopted country of Iran suffer? This is Khomeini trying to keep his revolution alive with this war since in peacetime he has no agenda, no mandate, no plan...nothing to offer Iran but misery.* Little did I know the Silent War was to be fought for eight years in which a million Iranian youth died and Saddam Hossein was egged on and armed by the USA. Dr. Buehler, a Viennese doctor who had performed the surgery on my friend Touss's knee for bone cancer, voluntarily went to Iran and fitted out hundreds of amputees from that war with prostheses. I wonder how all these real politique bastards who say that Saddam served our needs at the time would feel if something like this ever happened to us?

By September I was back in Washington, DC, staying with my parents and trying to figure out how to pick up the pieces of my life when I received a phone call from Robert Ode.

A mutual friend of ours had referred him to me. He said that he had been called out of retirement to go to our Tehran Embassy to help give out visas, and what did I think of the situation over there? I told him that the situation was not stable and advised him not to go; 444 days later his wife still hadn't heard from him. He was the senior diplomat of the group taken hostage.

What most people don't know is that the entire staff of the US Embassy, including a gorgeous Pakistani nurse friend of Neil and I named Stella, had been rotated out and sent back to the States because they had been through so much already, and so all the people who were taken hostage had only been in country 2 weeks.

I can also tell you that there were mile long lines outside the US Embassy of Iranians trying to get visas to come to the US, and this was quite an embarrassment to the revolutionaries that so many people wanted to leave. Contrary to the pundits who came up with conspiracy theories that Reagan had control over the hostage situation and timed their release for his election, my simple theory is that the revolutionaries took the embassy in order to stop the bad press that the mile long lines of people trying to emigrate, who were voting against them with their feet, was giving them.

Neil was back in San Francisco, working as a manager of an engineering group at the phone company by day and studying law at night, having decided to become a gay rights advocate, but his life was cut short at age forty by AIDs. Stella called us from Beverley Hills where she was a nurse for some psychiatrist! Touss stopped talking to me for twenty years because I wouldn't help him with a referral for a job in Saudi Arabia in an American firm, but then he went on to an OPEC appointment in Vienna. As a result of Chapter Eight of these Tales from the Zirzameen, a friend and former boss of his located me and together in a day and a half we relocated Touss. He and I are now in regular communication.

Photo by Alain DeJean, Sygma Corbis, gun battle

Photo by Alain Keler, Sygma Corbis, Neighborhood militia barricade

Photo by Hatami, Polaris Images, manning the barricades.

Photo by Hatami, Polaris Images, Fallen Comrade.

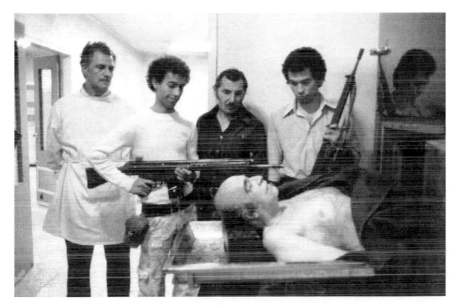

Photo by Abbas, Magnum Photos, late P.M. Hoveida

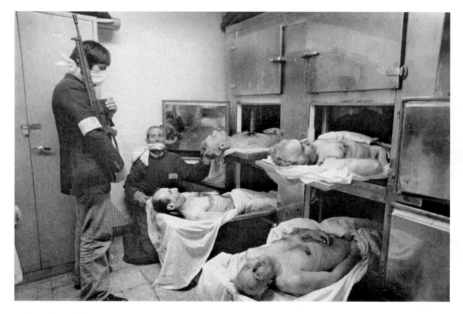

Photo by Abbas, Magnum Photos, late General Khosrodad, upper left, and other Generals of the Shah

Photo by Abbas, Magnum Photos, "Magh bar Shah," death to the King.

Photo by Hatami, Polaris Images "Farewell to Childhood...Looking back."
Women marching outside US Embassy while hostages inside.

EPILOGUE

Return to Iran

NOT ONLY WAS I ABLE TO REUNITE WITH MY LONG LOST FRIEND TOUSS Sepehr after 20 years and meet his wife and children for the first time in Europe but another unusual incident occurred two months ago. I received a phone call from a woman named Melody, in Los Angeles, who told me that after reading my story she had reason to believe that the woman, Pouran, whom I described as saving me from my hostage situation, was the mother of her best friend, Hormoz, who had been separated from her in a divorce when he was 8 months old and raised by his grandparents in L.A. He now lived in Seattle and wanted to talk to me. I had no idea that Pouran had a son. I had only known her little daughter Arian, 30 years ago when she was two. I asked him what he remembered hearing about his mom from his grandparents. He mentioned that they told him he had a half sister, who had gone to Spain for eye surgery when she was a little girl. I had been the one who had told Pouran to take her daughter to Madrid to Dr. Ramon Castroviejo for that surgery, since he was the best and I had gone to school in Rome with his children. Dr. Castroviejo had invented the corneal transplant. Now I was sure that Pouran was Hormoz's mom and he asked me to help him to find her. I asked my friend Fatema Soudavar Farmanfarmaeeian, in London, If she knew Pouran and her whereabouts. She had only met her once at a party at Fatema's house, but remembered her quite vividly because she had been tossed in their swimming pool with all her clothes on by some of her prankster friends and she had provided her a set of dry clothes to go home in.

Fatema, eventually recalled that she had two cousins in London but they were on vacation in Portugal. Then she recalled that they had a friend, Lady Renwick, who would know everything and she contacted her. From Lady Renwick, we learned that Pouran had passed away from heart failure seven years ago. We also learned that Pouran had another daughter named Mana who was the eldest of her three children, who had been raised by her grand-mother in Shiraz. Each of these children had come from a different marriage. Arian was the only one who Pouran had raised herself. Pouran had been married a total of seven times.

To make a long story short I was able to get the phone numbers exchanged and on the 7th anniversary day of Pouran's death, her two daughters were reunited with their long lost brother. From Mana I learned that not only had Pouran been related to Court Minister Allam, which I already knew, but that her uncle had once been married to the Shah's oldest sister Princess Ashraf and indeed Pouran's grand father had been the famous Prime Minister Ebrahim Ghavvam of Shiraz, who had once been the proprietor of Bagh Eram Gardens there.

On July 15th of 2008, I went to Iran after an absence of 30 years since the revolution. I wanted to get closure on this episode of my life. I stayed in the former Hilton where I had been captured. It is now called the Esteglal (freedom, sovereignty) Hotel. It was wonderful to see so many of my old friends like no time had passed at all and Tehran still had the old magic and the new. There were 30,000 trees that had been planted since I left, and I have never seen such a green city in my life. Also I definitely had the feeling that Iranians were in charge of Iran now, not foreigners, but that they still loved Americans. Everyone I talked to wanted peace with the USA and everyone wanted to practice their English with me. If I had had 3 months rather than ten days, it still would not have been enough time to see all my friends. That very first night I called Arian and she sounded just like her mom. She said" Get a taxi and come to our house right now!" It was 1 AM but I knew there was no point arguing and her mom had often given me the same order.

When I left she was two, now she is 32, happily married and with a very cute little 2 year old boy of her own.

One half hour before I had to depart for the airport, Sharokh, his two little daughters and his older sister Kayvan, came by to see me with Kavous, Touss's younger brother and the mischief maker of our Pietro Della Valle Film. I hadn't seen Sharokh and Kayvan in 40 years and hadn't seen Kavous in 30 years. It was like no time had passed at all.

Once again like deja vous, I found myself crying all the way to the airport, but this time it was the new Imam Khomeini Airport and not Mehrabad Airport which is presently reserved for domestic flights.

I now knew that the immense love in my heart for Iran is not just a thing of the past.

Arian in her home in Tehran, July 2008

Arian, me and her son, Nikarta, Tehran, July 2008

Hormoz and his daugther, Seattle 2000

Pouran's eldest daughter, Mana

Cyrus, Touss, me, Amir, their living room, 2005

Cyrus, Touss and Amir, Vienna, OPEC HQ, lobby, 2006

Amir, Touss and Cyrus, Vienna 2006

Cyrus, me, Amir, 2004, Vienna

NOTES AND BIBLIOGRAPHY

Pezeshkzad, Iraj. *My Uncle Napoleon*. Washington, DC: Mage Publishers, 2000. See pg. 33.

Ansary, Parvin. *The Travels of Pietro Della Valle*. 1975 documentary based on the diary of fifteenth century Italian traveler in Iran. See pg. 33.

Ansary, Parvin *Sarah-e Salmanih*. 1976 film starring Shohreh Aghdashloo. See pg. 32.

Other writing by Brian H. Appleton

CASMII Magazine (Campaign Against Sanctions and Military Intervention in Iran)
http://www.campaigniran.org/casmii/index.php?q=node/3499\
http://www.campaigniran.org/casmii/index.php?q=node/3015

Hack Writers Magazine
www.hackwriters.com/Eygpt2.htm
http://www.hackwriters.com/Torniella.htm

Irandockht Magazine
http://www.irandokht.com/forum_support/forumarticles.php?forumID=4&sectionID=58
http://www.irandokht.com/editorial/index4.php?area=pro&sectionID=46&editorialID=31

The Iranian Times Magazine
http://www.iranian.com/Appleton/2003/December/Ansary/index.html
http://www.iranian.com/Appleton/2004/April/Film/index.html

The Payvand News Magazine
http://www.payvand.com/news/07/feb/1161.html
http://www.payvand.com/news/07/mar/1103.html

The Persian Heritage Quarterly Magazine
http://www.persian-heritage.com/currentissue/index.asp?action=
archives.html

The Persian Mirror Magazine
http://www.persianmirror.com/Article_det.cfm?id=827&getArticleCate-
gory=41&getArticleSubCategory=3
http://www.persianmirror.com/Article_det.cfm?id=828&authorid=117&get
ArticleCategory=41&getArticleSubCategory=3

Life In Italy Magazine
http://my.lifeinitaly.com/search.php?searchid=84526
http://my.lifeinitaly.com/showthread.php?t=2079&highlight=Hills+Flo-
rence

INDEX